BIBLICAL MEDITATIONS
FOR ADVENT
AND THE CHRISTMAS SEASON

ALSO BY CARROLL STUHLMUELLER:

Biblical Meditations for Lent
Biblical Meditations for the Easter Season
Biblical Meditations for Ordinary Time
    (Weeks 1–9)
Biblical Meditations for Ordinary Time
    (Weeks 10–22)
Biblical Meditations for Ordinary Time
    (Weeks 23–34)

Biblical Meditations
for Advent
and the Christmas Season

by
Carroll Stuhlmueller, C.P.

Introduction by
Most Rev. Thomas J. Gumbleton
Auxiliary Bishop of Detroit

PAULIST PRESS
New York/Ramsey

Library of Congress
Catalog Card Number: 80-82083

ISBN: 0-8091-2318-5

Published by Paulist Press
545 Island Road, Ramsey, N.J. 07446

Printed and bound in the
United States of America

Contents

PART FOUR—Sundays and Feastdays of the Christmas
Season

With love and gratitude
to
my grandparents,
uncles and aunts
for the strength and inspiration
of our families

Foreword

This book of meditations breathes the winter–spring atmosphere of Advent and Christmas. Just as at winter time the sap settles into the roots of trees, our Advent reflections rest with our ancestors and origins. Yet the Christmas hopes of a new spring are astir and draw our thoughts upward into the branches and vines where new life germinates. At times, then, Advent and Christmas leave us composed within the warm earth and at other times within the brisk caress of the spring wind, reaching us from distant places.

In the biblical readings for the First Sunday of Advent ("A" cycle) the spirit of spring is enveloping us and we see a vision of foreign nations streaming toward Jerusalem from the distant ends of the earth. Once they arrive at the holy city, swords are beaten into plowshares and we begin turning the soft earth for a new planting. Suddenly, however, the tranquil setting is shattered; the procession stops! We are startled by "signs in the sun, the moon and the stars" ("C" cycle). We are about to witness the wondrous manifestation of a Savior.

Yet we must settle into our roots again. During the afternoon Mass of December 24, we meditate upon the genealogy of Jesus. We hear that "Abraham was the father of Isaac, Isaac the father of Jacob. . . ."

While Advent invites us to live with our ancestral hopes, it also alerts us that the genealogy is pregnant with wonderful life. A new generation is about to appear. New life, in fact, will be experienced within our very own selves. "He will save us through the baptism of new birth and renewal by the Holy Spirit. [We] become heirs, in hope, of eternal life" (Christmas Mass at Dawn).

The meditations in this book seek to preserve the winter–spring tension of Advent–Christmas, a spirit of returning to the sources of our life, a spirit awakening to new possibilities of "kindness and love" (Christmas Mass at Dawn). Our minds and hearts are nudged to be active and are quieted into contemplation. By means of such opposite pulls, biblical meditation finds its best moments and brings an ever more intense awareness of God's immediate but mysterious presence.

God has become incarnate in our midst, not so much in *this* or in *that* but in the relationship between the two, in the bonds that attract nations from afar toward Jerusalem, in the idyllic hope that "the calf and the young lion shall brouse together, with a little child to guide them" (Second Sunday of Advent, "A" cycle).

These meditations like those in two preceding volumes for Lent and the Easter Season do not seek conclusions from a biblical passage. Rather they encourage us to wait for the voice of the Spirit in between the two or three biblical passages of the eucharistic liturgy, in fact in between scriptural readings, the reality of our contemporary world and our own individual person. "Where two or three," Jesus said, "are gathered in my name, there am I in their midst" (Matt 18:20). "Wait! Be watchful in prayer!"

In order to alert us to God's mysterious presence in the warm depths of our roots and in the cool hopes of our branches and vines, each meditation is preceded by a summary or better by a significant idea from the biblical passages of each weekday and Sunday of Advent and the

Christmas season. These resumes cannot take the place of reading the entire passage from the Bible. Moreover each reader will hopefully add another important idea of his own so as to renew the healthy tension of God's mysterious, *relational* presence in our midst. The concluding prayer for each meditation is usually drawn from the antiphonal response after the first reading of the eucharistic liturgy. Between December 17 and 24 the famous "O" antiphons of afternoon vespers inspire the prayer.

These meditations were composed within the happy setting of Ein Karim, a village just west of Jerusalem where I was teaching for fifteen weeks. I am grateful to St. John's University School of Theology, Collegeville, Minn., for developing this program of study in the Holy Land, to the Catholic Theological Union at Chicago for cooperating in its fall semester, to Fr. Luke Steiner, O.S.B., director and fellow professor, and to all the participants, lay persons, seminarians, priests and religious. At Ein Karim and throughout the Holy Land we relived the Bible in a contemplative spirit with prophetic challenge.

I also express my gratitude to Ms. Shirley Moore, faculty secretary, and to Sister Kathleen Sheskaitis, I.H.M., graduate assistant at the Catholic Theological Union, for their invaluable help in typing and proofreading. Further assistance came from Sister Leonette Ternes, O.P., and Sister M. Eulalia Wagner, O.S.B. Finally I acknowledge the important role of Robert Heyer and Donald F. Brophy in the editorial office of Paulist Press.

Carroll Stuhlmueller, C.P.
The Catholic Theological Union at Chicago

Introduction

Many are turning to Sacred Scripture each day for their daily prayer and finding it more and more a way of integrating their very active lives with at least the beginnings of genuine contemplation.

For any who are doing this, or who might be inclined to do this, I think this most recent book of Carroll Stuhlmueller will prove to be invaluable.

It focuses on the daily liturgical readings of the Advent and Christmas season. Anyone who uses these helps to contemplative prayer will wish that there were more. But all will agree, I think, that prayer based on the experience of Advent, leading to the celebration of Christmas, is many times the most fruitful and almost effortless prayer we do.

Father Stuhlmueller's meditations are a very unobtrusive and yet most helpful guide for exploring and experiencing the rich truths we celebrate in faith during this time. They invite, they don't dictate. They allow us the opportunity to take this special season and build on it.

You might not think that this would be necessary. You wouldn't think that we needed any help to remind us that the Lord is coming, that he's just around the corner, waiting, watching, silent. But let's face it—all of us need reminders. All of us need an open hand and a calm voice bidding us to come and see. I would invite you to come and see, to wait alone or with someone, to listen with these meditations for something that is beyond all telling. It is an invitation to wait for the Lord.

When I stop to think about it, I know that all of life is an advent, a waiting for something we're not completely sure of, but which we want desperately, as much as life itself.

But we are not good waiters. We're not used to it. We have instant coffee, microwave ovens, split-second copy makers, and an instant-on mechanism on our TV sets. We can press the right buttons on machines and instantly we have the world at our fingertips. Waiting has become an obsolete enterprise for so many people. But not for all. Children's excitement builds while they're waiting. Expectant mothers wait for nine long months and are conscious of all the changes that are going on within their bodies and within their hearts. Old people wait for spring and often they wait to die. All of these experiences and many more can teach us something about the good that can come from waiting.

And this is precisely what Father Stuhlmueller does. He helps us to experience the good that can come from waiting. His thoughts on Advent show us how to wait, not with anxiety but with hope and anticipation. They give us a refreshing approach to the season of waiting, and they remind us that Advent is never a disappointment. The waiting is good, but it is never better than the event of Christ's birth. Our expectations and our hopes are never dashed by his coming. As the people of the Old Testament waited and were finally rewarded, so are we.

And for a lot of reasons, we need to be assured that the waiting is good. We need somehow to know that the things we cannot achieve instantly, such as justice for all persons and world peace, are really worth waiting and working for. There are times when we don't believe it.

There are times when the struggle becomes too much, the disappointments too frequent. When we try with our lives to preach the good news in a broken world, a part of us gets broken too. It is not difficult to recall numerous incidents where men and women give up, or turn in on themselves and on each other. It happens in marriages that have become stale; it happens in prisons that have become inhuman. It happens in governments that have forgotten or ignored the cries of people who are poor and hungry and oppressed. It happens among those involved in the peace movement, especially if it has been for a long time. It can be so frustrating to work long and hard for something that seems just beyond reach. When world events such as the building of nuclear weapons, racial tension, hunger and embassy takeovers are all around us, the threat of global destruction becomes so real that the waiting and the working for peace seem foolish to some. But waiting is good and not foolish. It is this time spent for the cause of right that makes the waiting worthwhile and redemptive. As Father Stuhlmueller prays in his meditation:

"Lord, strengthen me to wait upon you with courage and faith."

There is no better season to appreciate the benefits of waiting than Advent and Christmas. And I am glad and grateful that Father Stuhlmueller has helped me to "wait upon the Lord with courage and faith." What a difference there is between spending time for a good cause and waiting to see what the Lord has done for those who seek to make his world better!

✝ Thomas J. Gumbleton
Auxiliary Bishop of Detroit

PART ONE

Weekdays of Advent

Monday, First Week of Advent

Is 2:1–5. Many peoples shall stream toward Mount Zion, to receive peace, light and instruction.

Is 4:2–6.* Jerusalem will be a refuge for the remnant of God's people. The wonders of the exodus out of Egypt, symbolized by the smoking cloud, will be experienced again.

Matt 8:5–11. The Roman centurion, asking Jesus to cure his servant, protests that he is not worthy for Jesus to enter under his roof. In amazement Jesus sees people come from the East and the West and recline with Abraham, Isaac and Jacob.

The weekday readings of Advent begin with Isaiah's vision of universal peace. Centuries ago, while the Bible was still in the process of formation, this vision opened the book of Isaiah. Chapter two in fact has its own introduction: "This is what Isaiah, son of Amoz, saw concerning Judah and Jerusalem." Chapter one, with a more elaborate introduction, was added later, drawing its material from various moments of the prophet's long career. In some ways, therefore, the introductory vision, recorded in the opening lines of Chapter two, summarized the finest hopes and ultimate goal of Isaiah, son of Amoz.

This vision is found again, almost identically, in the prophecy of Micah (Mic 4:1–3). It is difficult to decide which prophet is the original author; there is even the possibility that each drew upon a popular, liturgical piece. In the latter case this vision represented a vague but wonderful hope that all nations and races would reunite harmoniously with full human dignity at the Jerusalem temple. This vision seemed almost too good to be

* For Year "A"

true, for it clashed with the regulations of the Jerusalem temple; it also seemed too good to be practical, for can all the peoples of the world really get along peacefully with one another? The final verse, added by Isaiah, restricts the pilgrimage to the "House of Jacob," while Micah seems even more restraining. Micah declared that while other peoples walk "in the name of their god . . . [Israel] will walk in the name of the Lord."

This narrowing of the vision is more than an exercise in biblical scholarship. We are told, indirectly but emphatically, that the universal hopes of this vision exact severe demands. We too will tend to restrict its meaning.

God's expectations can be measured in all their fierce and wonderful possibilities by the simple questions. Are we willing to invite to our family dinner table everyone who receives Holy Communion with us at church? Are we ready to forget injuries and grudges, forgive unkind words and actions—as we beat swords into plowshares and spears into pruning hooks? Yet this vision with which we begin Advent sweeps far beyond the boundaries of our parish or neighborhood. "All nations," therefore people of all different races and ethnic groups are streaming toward the Jerusalem temple. Again we ask, are we willing to open the doors of our home and welcome all these many different peoples? Really, it is too good to be true and hardly very practical.

How do we start? How can we take at least a few small steps away from our fears and prejudices toward this universal vision of peace? In the Gospel, Jesus was invited to the home of a Roman centurion, a man of a much different religion and ethnic background, a representative of a foreign, oppressive invader. And Jesus accepted. Then the Roman hesitated; he was totally unworthy of Jesus' presence within his home. Jesus was amazed at such gentle humility. Jesus too could not miss the centurion's solicitude for his slave who would have been a non-Roman from some captured nation. The Roman centurion was humbling himself before Jesus, a Jew, for the sake of his slave!

Jesus pointed to this outsider as an example of a genuine follower and descendant of Abraham, Isaac and Jacob. Today Jesus is advising us to look toward the outsider for direction and encouragement in becoming his true follower. People are streaming toward Jesus, our Zion and Jerusalem, our center of prayer and worship, and to our surprise we have been considering them outsiders. Jesus is saying to us: "I assure you, I have never found this much faith" in your midst.

During Advent we are asked to learn, humbly and gratefully, from the outsider how to live worthily inside the holy temple of God. From unexpected sources we can be taught so much. But we must not put any restrictive clauses on this vision, as happened in the book of Isaiah and particularly of Micah. It may be too good for now, but nonetheless it is necessary to keep our hopes as pure and exalted as possible, for even then they will be only a glimmer of what God really wants.

During Advent, we find the school of faith in such simple sources as the birth of a child. These details of life are neither inspired nor revealed; they existed before religion and sacred tradition ever started! The mysteries of our faith, then, can be illumined by the normal, natural marvels of daily life.

Let us begin to look toward strangers and forgotten people for the path that leads toward Jesus, our Zion and Jerusalem. Let us recognize in our family and neighborhood the models for divine inspiration. These will break down barriers. Such simple moments as conception and birth remove all differences.

Prayer:

I rejoice when I hear them say: let us go to the
house of the Lord.

Lord, do not allow the joy of this moment to be
tarnished by prejudice.

Let us live happily in the vision of seeing strangers,
infants, non-believers, and all the world moving
toward the center of all life, you, Lord Jesus.

Tuesday, First Week of Advent

Is 11:1–10. The Spirit of the Lord rests upon the seemingly dead root of Jesse, David's father, and a delicate new
life appears surrounded by paradise.

Luke 10:21–29. Jesus rejoices in the spirit at what is revealed to little ones, a vision which kings and prophets
longed to see.

Isaiah announced the work of the Spirit and Jesus
rejoiced in it. This Spirit seems fragile and tender. If we
judge from these two passages of Isaiah and Luke, the
Spirit leads to a scene of paradise where "the calf and the
young lion shall browse together, with a little child to
guide them." Such "fairy tales" are hidden from the
learned and the clever [and] revealed to the merest children. Yet fairy tales impart a lesson of profound conse-
quence to adults. These grown-ups can even be the
"prophets and kings [who] wished to see what you see . . .
and to hear what you hear."

The passage from Isaiah may seem as innocent as a
fairy tale, yet beneath its simple images a terrifying truth
is hidden. The image of "the stump of Jesse and . . . his
roots" tells us that the mighty Davidic dynasty has been

cut down like a tree to the ground. Nothing remains but a dry stump and some hidden roots. When this tree had been cut down by the Babylonians in 587 B.C. the people were shocked into the realization that the Davidic dynasty was really not eternal. Yet, through the prophet Nathan God has assured David: "your house and your kingdom shall endure forever before me; your throne shall stand firm forever" (2 Sam 7:16). What they had believed from the obvious meaning of these words was not what God intended. In shock the author of Psalm 89 cried out: "You have rejected and spurned ... your anointed. ... You have hurled his throne to the ground. ... How long, O Lord? (Ps 89:39, 45, 47).

The prophet could not repudiate the tradition of the Davidic dynasty. God must always be true to his word. The dynasty in some way will revive. The spirit of the Lord will rest upon the stump and the roots of Jesse.

That same Holy Spirit is now resting upon us and especially upon those parts of ourselves which seem dead and maybe betrayed. We must believe that God inspires no honorable desire nor offers any promise that will not be fulfilled. Yet the accomplishment of these divinely placed ideals will often enough come about in ways that we can never imagine. We should never restrict God by our understanding of his promises.

Right here we see the reason behind the fairy tale that follows in Chapter 11 of Isaiah. Perhaps the calf and the young lion will never browse together. Perhaps babies should never be allowed to play by the cobra's den. Yet the dream of universal peace and gentle trust is so wonderful that not even our fairy tales adequately measure up to it! When our faith dreams in these fantastic ways, Jesus rejoices in the Holy Spirit and says: "I offer you praise, O Father, Lord of heaven and earth, because what you have hidden from the learned and the clever you have revealed to the merest children."

Only strong and dedicated adults can remain persons of faith when their "Davidic dynasty" is cut down and nothing seems to remain of their hopes. All of us have lived through such harrowing experiences. What we were convinced was very good and inspired by God turned out to torture us with frustration. All of us who have dreamed our best dreams have felt betrayed by what we considered our very best! People who hope for little, lose little and suffer less. Our best and most unselfish hopes, which provide every evidence of being from God, let us down the hardest.

When we are "hoping against hope" (Rom 4:18) then we glimpse what kings and prophets longed to see but did not see. Somehow or other by faith we secretly realize that deeply imbedded in our losses there abides a potential for goodness beyond our imagination.

When married people are unable to have their own children or when they lose their only child in death, they must believe that their divinely inspired ideals of a family will be fulfilled in ways beyond the seeming powers of nature. When women and men follow God's call into consecrated celibacy, their ability and desire for intimate love and for their own children are not simply sacrificed like innocent lambs before a strange deity who asks the denial of what he creates and blesses.

It seems that when we have done our best, that best must collapse so that God's dreams for us may be fulfilled. Only when we offer to God our best spontaneously with full risk of not knowing the consequences, can God transform us beyond our fairy tales and wildest imagination. At the heart of our existence then lies a mystery which no one knows except Jesus and the heavenly Father—"and anyone to whom the Son wishes to reveal" it. This mystery is Jesus himself, a child stripped of divinity to communicate God to us, a human being destined to be stripped of humanity on the cross of death to reveal how we ought to live.

Isaiah declared that "the earth shall be filled with knowledge of the Lord as the water covers the sea." The mystery of who we are teems all around us. Like a child—like Jesus—we must rejoice in the Holy Spirit.

Prayer:

Lord, grant us the strength to dream out our best thoughts, the heroism to persevere through their collapse, the childlikeness to be reborn anew so that the mystery of your hopes be manifest in our lives. No life, lost in you, is ever lost, only transformed into its most mysterious possibility.

Wednesday, First Week of Advent

Is 25:6–10. On his holy mountain God provides a banquet for all peoples. Death is destroyed and tears are wiped away. We behold our God to whom we looked for salvation.

Matt 15:29–37. Jesus cured people of many infirmities and multiplied bread lest they collapse on the way home.

The dream and great hope expressed by Isaiah is fulfilled in the Gospel miracles of Jesus. Jesus overcame death when he cured "cripples, the deformed, the blind, the mute and many others besides." He laid out a magnificent banquet, multiplying loaves and fishes for common people who had followed him three days into the wilderness. Jesus asked them no questions ahead of time; he did not challenge their religious affiliation or ceremonial purity. He acted out of compassion:

> My heart is moved with pity.... By now they
> have been with me three days, and have nothing
> to eat. I do not wish to send them away hungry.

During Advent we are led by God into the wilderness. Each Old Testament reading touches new hopes and stirs greater longing. None of these movements of the spirit will be frustrated. Seeing us, Jesus will be moved with pity.

The reading from Isaiah, like the one for Monday of this first week of Advent, is one of those unusual passages that leaps out of its context and articulates hidden desires far ahead of their time. Very few Old Testament passages open salvation to all nations and races. The fact that Israel's religion rested upon the exodus out of Egypt and the covenant on Mount Sinai, that is, upon the doctrine of the election, leaves the Egyptians and other foreigners behind. The "non-elect," at best, remain in a kind of limbo. Yet, in this passage foreigners are called to be a part of Israel, just as in Monday's reading they are invited to participate in the temple ceremonies at Jerusalem.

Still another unusual hope is expressed by this passage from Isaiah. God "will destroy death forever." For most of the Old Testament death marked the end of personal, conscious existence. People survived in their offspring and in the destiny of their nation. Texts like the one in Psalm 6 occur often enough:

> For among the dead no one remembers you;
> In the nether world who gives you thanks? (Ps. 6:6).

Yet, as Israel was forced into contact with foreign nations, she began to appreciate their goodness and sincerity. Such is the conclusion reached in the books of Ruth and Jonah. As Israel had to face the mammoth problem of death striking the young, the innocent and even large numbers of people during the Babylonian destruction of Jerusalem, the people could not remain content with the traditional doctrine of election and of death. Individual texts like this one for Wednesday of the first week of Advent broke rank and expressed hopes long submerged or suppressed. God will certainly tear down the barriers between people and even the barrier between time and eternity.

Even in the days of Jesus these barriers were visibly present in the thinking of many people. The priestly Sadducees would not accept the resurrection of the body (Acts 23:6–8). Paul was opposed by a strong faction of Jewish disciples of Jesus who insisted that foreigners first become Jews if they are to be baptized as Christians (Gal 2). It takes a long time for great hopes to be accepted by people at large and at times by ourselves individually.

Each of us possesses ideas and hopes which may frighten us. We long to be a friendly brother or sister with everyone we meet. Yet we are afraid to take the risk, go into the wilderness and look to Jesus for direction and nourishment. We all believe that Jesus can work miracles. Yet, if we are striken with a crippling illness and especially if we face death, fear throws up many barriers and our faith seems to vanish from sight. In that wilderness we are not conscious of Jesus' presence. We panic! Like the disciples, we exclaim: It is hopeless! How could we ever get enough bread in this deserted spot to satisfy such a crowd?

Advent is a special period of prayer and recollection.

We are asked by the Church to set aside more time than usual in order to live more intensively in God's presence. We are training ourselves to look ever more keenly and continuously toward Jesus. By fasting and self-denial we feel even within our body as well as within our spirit how weak we are and how much we depend upon Jesus. Jesus in turn must look at us with pity and think how we will collapse on the way if he does not provide miraculous food.

Advent then encourages us to let our hidden hopes and desires lead us beyond our normal routine day-by-day existence. As we listen to the Scriptures, secret possibilities come to the surface. We allow ourselves to break loose from our ordinary context of life; we risk reaching beyond our normal, safe solutions. We leap over such barriers as racial or social divisions. We even survive death.

Each Eucharist during Advent ought to fulfill Isaiah's dream of "a feast of rich food and choice wines." The sacred ceremony ought to "destroy the veil that veils all peoples" in prejudices and fears. Holy Communion unites us to all who have died. It "will wipe away the tears from all faces."

"This is the Lord for whom we looked"—he is born in our midst. We have prepared well for Christmas during this Advent.

Prayer:

Lord, you are coming and will not delay. You will bring every hidden hope to light and reveal yourself in these secret inspirations. Lead us into the wilderness and have pity on us.

Thursday, First Week of Advent

Is 26:1–6. Jerusalem, a new city, is built by God as a
    home for the lowly and for those who trust in him.
Matt 7:21,24–27. Only those who do the will of God will
    be saved; they build their house on rock and it will not
    be swept away.

The biblical readings for this day set up a double
movement. In Isaiah God builds the city, setting up its
walls and ramparts to protect us; in the Gospel we build
the house solidly, setting it on rock. While Isaiah summons into the new city those who "trust in the Lord forever," Matthew repeats those sentences of Jesus which
reserve salvation "only [to] the one who does the will of
my Father in heaven." The Old Testament in this instance appears as the messenger of faith, and the New
Testament stresses action!

There is a line in the passage from Isaiah which
brings these divergent views back into harmony: "The
Lord is an eternal rock." We must return to this line, but
first we will pursue each of the two movements.

Insistence upon faith and trust in the Lord is a continuous motif throughout the prophecy of Isaiah. The
classic statement occurs in Chapter seven:

Unless your faith is firm
you shall not be firm!
(Is. 7:14)

Isaiah speaks from a time of crisis when Ahaz, King of
Jerusalem, had no alternative but to trust in God. He was
unable to muster an army and repel an invasion from the
northern kingdom of Israel. It was immoral to appeal to

Assyria for help because that meant becoming a vassal of this foreign power, losing national independence and gaining nothing in the long run. We, too, are faced with crises, at least at crucial moments of our lives, when to do anything would mean doing something immoral. We can see no good option or moral alternative. Isaiah warns and encourages us: "Be watchful and be tranquil; do not fear and do not let your courage fail." Isaiah later repeats these words in a meditative way:

> By waiting and by calm you shall be saved,
> in quiet and in trust your strength lies.
> (30:15)

The theme of faith is repeated in today's reading:

> Trust in the Lord forever!
> For the Lord is an eternal rock.

The Lord will surround us who have faith as he does the holy city with "walls and ramparts." And the Lord him-self *is* that city. He is the rock which sustains us. He is the Holy One, enshrined within us. There is a clash of images here! It means that the Lord is behind and before us, around about us and within us, supporting us from beneath, glorifying us from above.

> I love you, O Lord, my strength,
>   O Lord, my rock, my fortress, my deliverer.
> My God, my rock of refuge, my shield, the horn of
>   my salvation, my stronghold!
> Praised be the Lord (Ps 18:2–3).

And yet there are other moments in our life when we will be rightly condemned by God and our neighbors if we remain silent and motionless.

> There is an appointed time for everything. . . .
> a time to be born, and a time to die; . . .
>   a time to be silent, and a time to speak
> (Eccles 3:1, 7).

There is a time for action, when it simply is not enough to cry out: "Lord, Lord!" "Only the one," Jesus says, "who *does* the will of my Father in heaven" "will enter the kingdom of God." To do nothing is like building a house on sandy ground. Once the rainy season sets in, the water will lash at the foundation and the house will collapse.

Jesus says we should be "like the wise person who built his house on rock." Isaiah explains that "the Lord is an eternal rock." We must act but always through the strength and direction of the Lord, resting ourselves thoroughly upon Jesus. Only when each of our actions is directed by a conscious turning to the Lord for guidance, only when a sense of the Lord's presence accompanies us in all that we do, only then will there be an integral wholeness about life. Everything will fit together firmly. No single action will be out of harmony with the others nor disrupt the peace of our lives.

> A nation of firm purpose you keep in peace;
> in peace, for it trusts in you—writes Isaiah.

Whether we be silent or speak, remain motionless or act, we must be firmly rooted in the Lord. We must rest upon the rock of the Lord.

Prayer:

Lord, open to me the gates of justice. Teach me when to be silent. Yet in every moment let me take refuge in you and rest my confidence in you. Let me live always in your holy city; may you be the rock of my house.

Friday, First Week of Advent

Is 29:17–24. In a very little while God will wondrously complete his work of creation. No one will ever again be shamed; everyone will reverence the God of Israel.

Matt 9:27–31. Jesus gives sight to two blind men who were confident that he could do it, but he sternly warns them to tell no one. Nonetheless they spread the word through the whole area!

As we read this passage from Isaiah, we cannot help wondering if his poetic sense had run ahead of his common sense. Is he dreaming out loud as he writes:

> the deaf shall hear,
> the eyes of the blind shall see,
> the tyrant will be no more,
> Jacob shall have nothing to be ashamed of.

Something of the same impression comes upon us in reading the Gospel. Religion seems to turn into idyllic poetry and merits the charge of presenting "pie in the sky." Two blind men of Capernaum are cured by Jesus. The cynic will ask about the ninety-eight others who remained blind! Today, despite the miracles of Jesus there are many deaf people who do not hear, many blind who do not see, many tyrants across the earth, many just people put to shame. Isaiah stated that in "a very little while" all this misery would cease. Yet we are still waiting for this magnificent transformation.

The actions of Jesus may cast some light upon the phrase of Isaiah, "a very little while." Jesus did not cure the two blind men right away. They followed Jesus at some distance, all the while crying out, "Son of David, have pity on us!" They caught up with Jesus, only when he had arrived at the house where he was staying that night. Once Jesus touched their eyes, they were cured, not in "a very little while" but instantly. We too must follow Jesus with our desires and hopes.

Hopes enable us to appreciate what we receive and to love the one from whom we receive. What comes too quickly and too easily, is seldom appreciated properly. We take the giver for granted and tend to waste the gift. What is given to everyone at once reduces the action to mass production. The personal element is lost; we are preoccupied with impersonal things.

Jesus waited till the two blind men had "caught up with him." We too must seek *Jesus* rather than the gift easily put into our grasp. We must be convinced that Jesus can and will act for us out of loving compassion. He asked the two blind men: "Are you confident I can do this?" The personal interchange continued as they answered, "Yes, Lord!" At that he touched their eyes—gently, lovingly, beseechingly. Jesus can help us only when we confess a spontaneous faith in his goodness and allow him to touch us where we are weak and in need. As Jesus touched them, he said, "Because of your faith, it shall be done to you." At the moment when Jesus touches us, he reads deeply into our hearts for an expression of faith. We must be confident that his love will overcome every obstacle. In a true sense love is blind and sees none of the difficulties thrown into the way by fear and selfishness.

After curing the two blind men, "Jesus warned them sternly, 'See to it that no one knows of this.' " We would expect the opposite reaction. Why not throw a party so that the entire village can rejoice over the abundance of God's goodness! Yet, Jesus did not want his miracles to turn into a circus in which all personal concern is lost in feverish excitement. There are still other reasons for what is sometimes called the "messianic secret," Jesus' way of concealing his messianic identity. Jesus himself must become blind, deaf and dead, and rise from the dead, before the kingdom of God is at hand. Jesus must not just touch the eyes of the blind but totally share their condition.

As we search for Jesus, Jesus is one with us in our hopes and desires. With us Jesus is passing through his death to resurrection. The stronger is our desire to find Jesus and be restored to health and peace, the more urgent is Jesus' longing to cure us and transform our lives. The Gospels say that the blind men caught up with Jesus. They also imply that Jesus was seeking the blind in his yearning to help them. Jesus too was catching up with them. Yet Jesus would never short-circuit his work and perform miracles without a personal interchange. He did not come to work miracles but to seek those who were lost (Luke 19:10).

For Jesus to catch up with us, we need to have a faith that is obedient, loving, unconditional, open, seeking Jesus rather than what he can do for us, accepting Jesus confidently on his terms. We find Jesus only when we allow him to find us.

Once we are found and Jesus touches us, the prophet Isaiah's words come true. In that "very little while" there is an interchange of love and confidence—and we recover.

Prayer:

Lord, strengthen me to wait upon you with courage and faith. Let me seek one thing: to dwell in your house all the days of my life and there gaze upon your loveliness. Lord, cure my blindness that I might see your beauty.

Saturday, First Week of Advent

Is 30:19–21,23–26. The Lord binds up the wounds of his people, immediately answers their prayers, shows himself openly as their teacher and grants an abundance of good gifts.

Matt 9:35–38; 10:1,6–8. Jesus prays that there be many workers at harvest time. He sends the twelve to the lost sheep of the house of Israel.

The prophecy of Isaiah seems more adventurous than the gospel of Matthew in today's liturgy. The prophet implies the immediate presence of God:

No longer will your Teacher hide himself,
but with your own eyes you shall see your Teacher.

In Matthew's gospel Jesus' words seem more restrictive. Jesus sent forth the twelve to cure sickness and disease instead of performing these works of mercy himself. Isaiah's vision, moreover, sweeps universally across high mountains and lofty hill, across the heavens where "the light of the moon will be like that of the sun, and the light of the sun will be seven times greater." Matthew, on the contrary, confines the apostolate of the twelve to "the lost sheep of the house of Israel."

Jesus was no less adventurous than Isaiah. This son of Nazareth had a profound grasp of the Scriptures, especially Isaiah whom he quoted during his inaugural address in the hometown synagogue (Luke 4:16–22). We also know from the temptation scene how anxious Jesus was to break loose as soon as possible and to fulfill all the promises. More than anything else, however, Jesus was obedient to the will of his heavenly father; this compliance meant that Jesus followed the slow process of human development. Redemption basically consisted in the transformation of people rather than in the accomplishment of a mighty work. Therefore, Jesus had to adapt himself to the gradual turning of our mind and heart toward God.

The slow process of human development means that change begins and proceeds first within the family and neighborhood and only after a long time reaches out to the universe. Otherwise the growth becomes mechanical and impersonal. For this reason Jesus sent the twelve first to "the lost sheep of the house of Israel." It means that whatever each of us possesses ought to be shared at once within our family and neighborhood. "The gift you have received, give as a gift."

Within our family we pray to expel unclean spirits, as we continually exhort and inspire one another to purity of heart, spontaneous seeking of God's will and courageous acts of charity. Here too we "cure sickness and disease of every kind." We are solicitous about the welfare and good health of one another. We bear the burdens of one another.

The greater happiness and peace achieved within our family ought to make us all the more anxious to bring more and more friends, even distant acquaintances into our circle of love and compassion. What we possess becomes a model of what we want everyone to enjoy. Like Jesus our heart too ought to be "moved with pity." We pray all the more earnestly that God "send out laborers."

At this moment the spirit of Isaiah stirs within the hearts of some of our sons and daughters. These generous persons will be urged to go to foreign lands. Others will be caught up in profound prayer and seek a contemplative way of life. Others will be fired with hopes so adventurous as to seem impractical and unreal, as they see "the light of the moon . . . like that of the sun and the light of the sun . . . seven times greater!"

Although Jesus worked only with the house of Israel, nonetheless, he was continually giving hints and signals of his heart's desire to embrace the world. The adventurous missionaries with Isaiah's spirit keep alive similar hopes and desires in our hearts. At home we could become very selfish with all our good gifts, were it not for these laborers who go to the harvest areas of the world.

"The gift you have received, give as a gift." This Advent we prepare to celebrate the new birth of Jesus within our families and neighborhoods. May such good gifts close at home make us more anxious that this "Teacher no longer hide himself" but enable all men and women to see with their own eyes.

Prayer:

Come, Lord Jesus. Let us see your face and we shall be saved. Happy are all who long for your coming. May each of us be your instrument in stirring these desires among all our brothers and sisters.

Monday, Second Week of Advent

Is 35:1–10. The lame leap, the dumb sing, streams burst forth in the desert during the new exodus. God's people enter Zion rejoicing.

Luke 5:17–26. Jesus cures the paralytic and in the process also forgives his sins.

Again as on the Saturday of the first week of Advent, the prophet Isaiah sees a marvelous vision of the Lord's redeemed people. They are streaming across the desert, which now flows with fresh water, and the head of this triumphant procession is already entering Zion, the Holy City. Jesus, in the meanwhile, is caught in a petty theological argument. People overlook his ability to cure a paralytic in order to argue theology. At times like this, human sophistication collapses before the obvious wonder of God's ways!

Similar to last Saturday's meditation, we see that the transformation of the world must be celebrated in personal change of heart within a family setting. We do not know what Jesus was discussing, surrounded as he was by a large group of people as well as by "Pharisees and teachers of the law who had come from every village of Galilee and from Judea and Jerusalem." We are certain that confusion and consternation set in when several men made an opening in the roof and lowered a paralytic with his mat into the middle of the crowd.

Jesus abruptly stopped the theological discussion but immediately stirred up a hotter theological debate! He said to the paralytic: "My friend, your sins are forgiven you." Jesus could have been interpreted to mean nothing more than what anyone of us might say: How can there be sin in your heart when you seek the Lord this earnestly? All of us must forgive sins in this way, by recognizing the abundant charity or serious concern within our neighbor. But Jesus was also hinting that he was more than a human being.

For Jesus, moreover, the forgiveness of sin was to be linked with total concern for the other person. To show the full implication of spiritual transformation, Jesus cured the paralytic who then "stood erect ... picked up the mat he had been lying on and went home praising God."

We realize as well that the sacrament of reconciliation ought not to be confined exclusively to forgiving sins, but should extend into a dialogue for reconciling the penitent with neighbor and with all aspects of life.

The spiritual apostolate of the Church and of each member of the Church cannot be faithful to Jesus if it is confined to people's souls. To forgive sins requires that we be anxious to help the other person in all areas of his life. It requires that the Church take seriously the social sins of today's world and work vigorously to remedy social injustices.

At this point we turn to the prophecy of Isaiah:

> Strengthen the hands that are feeble,
> > make firm the knees that are weak,
> Say to those whose hearts are frightened:
> > Be strong, fear not!
> Here is your God,
> > he comes with vindication.

Isaiah did not announce the forgiveness of sin and then leave the people otherwise without home or protection. These lines probably come from the time of the Babylonian exile or still later. They were added to the prophecy of the earlier Isaiah as a confirmation of his hopes. If Jerusalem had fallen and the people were deported, as the first Isaiah threatened would happen, this suffering for sin was purifying and reinvigorating. The people would return from exile so gloriously that their songs would echo from the hills and mountains.

We too ought to be instruments of love, so that our kindliness toward the physical and material needs of others will induce a charity strong enough to burn away sin. The removal of sin ought to have repercussions across the total lives of others. Sometimes we may first address the sins and faults, at other times it will be more sensible to care first for the physical needs of others. Most of all we seek the full human dignity of our brothers and sisters.

The birth of Jesus ought to restore dignity and respect within the family. If we are worried about the faults and failings of others, Advent asks that we extend our concern over the totality of their lives and that we leave behind a vision of hope as did the prophet Isaiah.

Prayer:
Come to us, Lord, and bring us peace. Grant that this peace be rooted in hearts freed from sin and be manifest in concern for all the needs and worries of others.

Tuesday, Second Week of Advent

Is 40:1–11. God calls an unknown prophet to prepare the
way for the new redemption of his people from exile.
Matt 18:12–14. There will be more joy over finding the
one lost sheep than over the ninety-nine that did not
wander away.

There is a hidden part in each one of us. When it is
found by God, the Good Shepherd, it will be God's instrument for transforming our entire existence. All the
rest of ourselves will rejoice because the 99 percent of
ourselves will be transformed by this one percent. The
lost sheep is that buried, secluded or forgotten part within each of us.

A good example of the lost sheep is located in the
prophet-author of the first reading. This glorious announcement of a prophetic call originated in God's heavenly throne room. God called out (in the plural form of
the Hebrew verb) to the many celestial beings around his
throne: "Comfort, O comfort my people!" One after another these angelic creatures shout, as it were, to the
earth below:

> *First voice:* "In the desert prepare the way of the
> Lord!"
> *Second voice:* "Cry out."
> *Third voice:* "The grass withers ... [but] the
> word of our God stands forever."
> *Fourth voice:* "Cry out at the top of your voice."

A prophet of mighty ability responded from earth:
"What shall I cry out?" At God's reply this prophet began a prophetic career leading to the composition of the

Bible's golden poetry. Yet, the way of the Lord, which led the people back to their homeland, away from the Babylonian exile, turned out to be a way toward rejection and oblivion for the prophet. His name was forgotten; his exquisite poetry added to the scroll of the earlier prophet Isaiah. He turned out to be the lost sheep waiting to be found by the Lord.

Jesus and his early disciples turned to this prophet, not only to appreciate John the Baptist who prepared the way of the Lord, but also to remain at peace during the tragic death of Jesus by quoting passages like Chapter 42 and Chapter 53. The work of the "Great Unknown" remained lost within Israel till it was found by the Good Shepherd. Then it brought exceptional joy to the other ninety-nine.

Each person possesses hidden talents. We can all remember certain moments when another person discovered this buried part—this lost sheep within himself—and acted and responded in a way that took everyone, including ourselves, by surprise. At times a chance remark, an encouraging word, an accidental meeting, a sudden opportunity turned our life around. We began to act in a new way that profoundly affected our whole existence.

What is lost in ourselves or in others may have been buried into forgetfulness by a sinful action. Perhaps a sarcastic remark by ourselves or another, maybe a failure due to inappropriate or insufficient preparation, caused us or others to resolve never to try again. The sheep is lost in the wilderness. Or it is possible that some people just get lost in the shuffle. For one reason or another they are neglected by their parents or family, by their teachers or classmates. They end up without ambition or hope; they plod along, muted by the misfortunes of life.

Such people exist all around us. In fact, we may be a

lost sheep, or at least some part of ourselves may have
been buried deeply within our subconscious. Advent is
the time for us to prepare the way of the Lord, to redis-
cover the lost sheep in ourselves and in others.

If the "sheep" was lost through sin, then the search
will be more difficult. Along the way through the wilderness, we will be asked to forgive or to seek forgiveness. If
the "sheep" wandered away out of fright or out of simple
neglect, then it will be found only by tender concern.
This "sheep" may be very similar to oriental sheep,
which once lost lie down and remain where they are. The
lost part within ourselves or within others may stop
where it is, totally inactive. To be found, someone else
must take the initiative and actively pursue the "sheep."
Just as the discovery of Isaiah Chapters 40–55 as a separate book, distinct from the earlier section of the prophecy, was due to long, tedious research and serious
challenge, we too may be required to utilize modern
means like psychology, and most of all to persist perse-
veringly, humbly, positively.

Finally, some lost "sheep" are found only by the divine Good Shepherd, Jesus. We look forward to Christmas when Jesus steps anew into our lives to discover
hidden gifts, talents and hopes that can turn our lives
around.

Prayer:

The lost sheep is found. Let the heavens be glad and
the earth rejoice. The Lord is king ever more fully and
completely in our lives and we are ever more alive in the
depths of our heart, mind and whole self.

Wednesday, Second Week of Advent

Is 40:25–31. Those who hope in the Lord renew their
strength.

Matt 11:28–30. "Come to me," Jesus says, "all you who
are weary, and I will refresh you. My yoke is easy and
my burden light."

The Great Unknown, prophet of the Babylonian exile, was summoned by God to comfort and strengthen the
people, whose memories were haunted by the destruction
of their holy city, Jerusalem. Their family bonds as well
as their familiar ways of life had been shattered. They
were saying to the prophet:

My way is hidden from the Lord,
and my right is disregarded by my God.

As we read yesterday, God summoned this prophet to
comfort these desolate people and to announce their return to their own land along the "way of the Lord."

The prophet obediently responded to God, composing the melodious, sweet-sounding and richly theological
poems in Chapters 40–55. As he comforted the people, he
also stirred their hopes.

Ideals and ambitions can be very burdensome. At
times in a family one member is so driven by a single, ab-
sorbing goal or desire, that no one else in the family really counts any more. As a result, tensions develop, anger
flares, divisions set in. At the very least such hopes place
an oppressive and staggering burden on everyone.

Hopes, however, can also be liberating, uplifting and
productive of new life. Hopes that are not riveted on
things and actions but center upon persons tend to be

very encouraging. Such hopes take the burden from us. Such is the case when we hope *in the Lord.* In Isaiah we read:

> They that hope in the Lord will renew their
>   strength,
>   they will soar as with eagle's wings;
> They will run and not grow weary,
>   walk and not grow faint.

Whenever we hope in people, we strengthen them and so make their burden light. If we sense that someone has great hopes *in us*—not just in what we can do for them but rather *in us*—we are complimented and buoyed up. We feel that we can "soar as with eagle's wings!"

Such hopes *in people* have their risks! First of all, they lack the definite plan of action associated with hopes in what people can *do.* Whenever we lay out definite ideas, calculate each step and practice dry runs, we are not involved in "hopes." St. Paul wrote about such "hope" this way:

> Hope is not hope if its object is seen; for how is
> it possible for one to hope for what one sees?
> And hoping for what we cannot see means
> awaiting it with patient endurance (Rom 8:24–
> 25).

St. Paul's words here about "patient endurance" remind us again of the suffering and submission accepted by anyone who hopes *in people.* In marriage a man and a woman pledge their love with hopes in one another and particularly in their bond of union, yet they add at once the risk that they willingly accept: "for better or for worse, in sickness and in health." Hopes, therefore, risk everything—and high stakes—for a future that remains unclear, even unknown.

Yet when we truly put our hopes *in people* and are bonded with them in love, such risks bring excitement and adventure; they remove the danger of monotony. In such cases we "soar as with eagle's wings . . . [We] run and do not grow weary." This speed of response and this exhilarating excitement become all the more exuberant and noticeable, when the person in whom we hope is *the Lord.*

Then we who are weary will be refreshed. To take the burden of such risks upon ourselves and learn from Jesus, actually refreshes us. It is always a transforming experience to undertake a great work with someone who is "gentle and humble of heart." Truly in such situations, "my yoke is easy and my burden light."

Christmas, and the days of Advent in preparation for the feast, enable us to renew our loyalty to Jesus. We gather together all of our hopes and ambitions and place them in Jesus. We do not so much go after accomplishments as we seek the ever more intense presence of Jesus during our actions and responsibilities. Thus we carry the burden or yoke of Jesus, and it is light, refreshing and re-invigorating.

Prayer:

Lord, you are coming and will not delay. We can be certain that burdens will turn into secret joys, tired steps will raise themselves and move forward lightly. May we find all of our hope in you. Then we will be moved by you to place ever more hope in our family, community and neighborhood.

Thursday, Second Week of Advent

Is 41:13–20. The prophet anticipates a fearful threshing
of the mountains and offers a consoling message to the
poor and thirsty.
Matt 11:11–15. John the Baptist is Elijah, threatening to
burn every tree that does not yield fruit yet humbly
making way for the least in the kingdom of God.

Both biblical readings combine a double biblical tradition, one side of which announces a fiery judgment
while the other side suffers compassionately with the destitute. These two sides of biblical religion remain con-
stant throughout the ages. God is to be loved and feared!
(Deut 6:5,13). Jesus announced peace and brought the
sword (John 14:27; Luke 12:51–53). The clue to this unusual, almost contradictory combination lies in everyday
experience! In the entire animal kingdom, from the irra-
tional to the human, parental love surrounds its offspring
with *tender* concern and guards it *fiercely!*
Isaiah heard God address Israel with nicknames.
Like a father or a mother, God calls the infant Israel "my
little worm" and "my little maggot." These expressions
come naturally to mind as a parent looks down at a child
squirming in its arms. Understood in this way, the words,
"worm" and "maggot," are not demeaning toward Israel,
but they do surprise us when they come from the mouth
of God. We expect God to act with more proper dignity!
God is not afraid of sacrificing his divine stateliness to be
known as a loving and tender parent, but he will summon
every ounce of his omnipotence and with awesome wrath
defend the poor and the powerless. He will thresh mountains of evil so throughly that their dust will be carried
away by a strong wind.

A farmer tramples upon the harvested wheat, then throws the stalks into the air. The seed because it is heavier falls to the ground while the withered leaves and dried up stem are swept away by the wind. Threshing, we note, combines the heavy determination of stamping and beating with the easy rhythmic sweep of throwing the stalks into the air . . . just as God blends tenderness with strength.

The compassionate concern of God shows up beautifully in the second part of the Isaiah passage. Actually a new poem begins with: "The afflicted and the needy seek water in vain." Isaiah writes with extraordinary use of sound: for instance, the first line, just quoted, contains a continual use of *eem* sounds, so that the tone or resonance of the poor is echoed in the phrase "in vain." If they are still seeking, naturally they have not found! The second line which tells us about "tongues . . . parched with thirst" makes use of ever deeper guttural or throaty sounds, the dry *aah.* Mercifully God does not force such people to listen to a sacred speech. The Lord answers them with immediate action: "I open up rivers on the bare heights" and plant the seven sacred trees of paradise. We are reminded of the well-watered garden in Genesis 2:6,10–14

If any of us would actually witness this mighty transformation that makes the desert bloom and even the mountain ridges flow with water, we would not know whether to dance with reckless joy through the flowers and rainfall or to cover our face out of fearful disbelief and our inability to cope with it all. Again God blends tenderness with strength.

Jesus' words too combine gentleness with energetic power. He refers to newly born infants, the least in the kingdom of God, who are greater than the fierce proph-

ets, Elijah and John the Baptist. Jesus turns the coin over
and changes the metaphor to the violent who take the
kingdom by force. The weakest infant is stronger and better prepared to occupy the kingdom than Elijah and John
whose preaching attracted yet astonished and frightened
people. Nonetheless, an infant remains an infant, thoroughly dependent upon gentle care. The Gospel ends
with a serious warning: "Heed carefully what you hear!"

Everyone of us occasionally comes up against violent opposition. How are we to cope with it? Today's
reading asks us to respond with the consciousness of
Christmas and the presence of God as an infant. Our first
reply takes the form of prayer, patience and the willingness to be gentle. Giants can melt before a child, so powerful is the child in overcoming all opposition. Christmas
also directs our reaction in the way of sustained hope.
God can work miracles, and the most difficult miracle
must be the transformation of sin into goodness, of a desert into paradise. This second response of faith in miracles induces a healthy and awesome fear. Who among us
can deal with miracles? Finally, no matter what may
have been the delicate loveliness and the majestic grandeur of former ages, crumbled now under the disintegrat-
ing forces of sin, we must believe that the future will be
still more elegant and splendid. We will risk even our
show of force by acting humbly as a child, confident that
"the hand of the Lord will do something" new and that
"the Holy One of Israel will create it."

Prayer:

Lord, you make known your might and the glorious
splendor of your kingdom, yet our immediate and spontaneous response to all your actions is the lovely and encouraging refrain:

The Lord is kind and merciful,
slow to anger and rich in compassion.

Friday, Second Week of Advent

Is 48:17–19. I, the Lord, teach you and lead you on the
way ... if only you hearken to my commandments.
Then your prosperity will be like a river.
Matt 11:16–19. Both the austere John the Baptist and the
sociable Jesus are rejected.

We each prefer one way of life more than another,
and that is very normal. God created each one of us with
a distinctive personality, special preferences, individual-
ized vocations. Because we tend to become overly specialized with strong likes and dislikes, we badly need others
to complement what we are lacking. St. Paul even went
so far as to say that each of us must fill up what is lacking
in the body of Christ! Yet we tend to resist this advice; we
do not want to admit our weaknesses. We even become
defensive and then aggressive if others detect our inability
to perform or control.

This ability to fill in what is missing in any one of
us becomes the issue or main point of Jesus' words. Jesus
quoted a proverb which stated exceptionally well how we
need joyful people who dance readily and compassionate people always ready to sympathize. Yet each was
spurned and ridiculed:

We piped you a tune but you did not dance!
We sang you a dirge but you did not wail!

Jesus was leading up to the punch line.

John [the Baptist] appeared neither eating nor drinking, and people say, "He is mad!" The Son of Man appeared eating and drinking, and they say, "This one is a glutton and a drunkard, a lover of tax collectors and those outside the law!"

Many practical conclusions can be drawn from Jesus' words, but most of all he is pleading with us to give the other person a chance. We must not judge harshly nor condemn too quickly. Others have every right to that which God provides so plentifully and so freely—namely, *time.*

In Jesus we find the fullness of time (Eph 1:10). God prepared for that moment over centuries of sacred history. God is not on our back, reminding us each moment what to do and what not to do. God gives us space and time. A lifetime is normally a collection of all kinds of time, as the well-known poem in the book of Ecclesiastes states so simply and yet so emphatically:

There is an appointed time for everything,
    and a time for every affair under the
        heavens. . . .
A time to be born, and a time to die;
    a time to plant, and a time to uproot the plant
        (Eccles 3:1–8).

The contrasting lines continue over many verses.

We all need time to grow and thus to develop our own individual talents. We yearn to be encouraged and complimented, so that we can keep trying. Others must be patient and tolerant, overlooking mistakes, gently correcting, learning from us all the while.

As a community or family, we must be anxious to profit from all the talents in our midst—from those prompt to sympathize with our sorrows, from those who are austere, as well as from those who are more easygoing, sociable and even bounding outside the accepted norms. Jesus ate with tax collectors and others outside the law.

Jesus instructs us with his own ecumenical, patient spirit. He is the Lord, our God, teaching us what is for our good and leading us on the way we should go. As we combine these statements of the prophet in today's first reading with the will of Jesus, we understand what is the commandment to which we must hearken, the law which will make our prosperity overflow like a river and sweep forward like the waves of the sea. It is the commandment of love and unity. This, we know, was Jesus' first commandment (Matt 22:34–40).

If we remain united in love, we will be quick with patience and slow with judgment. We will persevere through all difficulties and give everyone the necessary time and space to grow and to make his contribution. We will feel a serious need for the help and contribution of others, all the more as we develop our own specialized talents. Only through others will we be truly balanced and integral in our values and attitude.

Jesus' final words appear so true: "Time will prove where wisdom lies."

Prayer:

We are waiting for our Savior, the Lord Jesus Christ. Born in our midst he followed our slow process of time and so transfigured our lowly bodies into copies of his own glorious body.

Saturday, Second Week of Advent

Sir 48:1–4,9–11. Destined to return before the day of the
   Lord, Elijah will restore unity among God's people.
Matt 17:10–13. John the Baptist was Elijah who suffered
   as Jesus will have to suffer. Jesus added that he himself
   was Elijah who will restore all things.

Elijah certainly caught the imagination of the Israelites. Because he was taken up from earth in a whirlwind
(2 Kgs 2:11), a tradition arose that he must return before
the great messianic day. The abruptness with which he
ended his days on earth corresponds well with his sudden
first appearance in the Bible. He stood without any formal introduction in the presence of King Ahab, announc-
ing a famine upon the land (1 Kgs 17:1). As we read the
account of Elijah from 1 Kings 17 to 2 Kings 2, he
seemed to be caught between violently contrasting scenes.
Tenderly he brought a dead boy back to life for the sake
of the widowed mother (1 Kgs 17:22), but in the very
next chapter he confronted four hundred and fifty false
prophets who were eventually brought down to the brook
Kishon where Elijah "slit their throats" in mass execution. Elijah, we see, can act with exceptional strength and
self-confidence, yet he can also be so discouraged as to
flee all the way to Mount Sinai to be consoled in a quiet
vision of the Lord's presence (1 Kgs 19).

While John the Baptist captured some of the more
austere and violent aspects of Elijah, Jesus saw himself
also in the role of Elijah the persecuted prophet who ush-
ers in "the great and terrible day" of the Lord (Mal 3:23).
As any notable tradition was transmitted in biblical
times, it tended to absorb the aspirations and hopes of
people of each generation. Elijah came to symbolize the

total transformation of Israel through God's exceptional intervention.

The liturgical reading from Sirach omits verses 5 to 8 of Chapter 48. More of the marvelous exploits of Elijah, enhanced by tradition to reflect the evolving messianic hopes of the people, are recorded by Sirach than we read at the eucharistic celebration. The liturgy wants to focus on a single great accomplishment of Elijah: to reestablish *unity* within the families and tribes of Israel.

> You are destined, it is written, in time to come to
> put an end to wrath before the day of the Lord,
> To turn back the hearts of parents toward their
> children, and to re-establish the tribes of Jacob.

We all recognize unity as *the* most difficult goal to achieve. If a serious division sets in between members of the same family, it seems impossible to restore love and agreement. When religious groups split off from one another, we end up with the overwhelming scandal of division within Christianity or the violent differences between Christianity, Judaism and Islam, three world religions sprung from the same parent and patriarch, Abraham.

Of themselves religious groups cannot arrive at unity. They must be prodded and forced by external forces, usually by secular or even irreligious coercion: i.e., godless communism, financial distress, loss of members, inability to address basic human needs.

The birth of Jesus, like a newly born child in a home otherwise split apart, can be one of those "natural" forces that bring about unity. Everyone loves infants; infants can attract all kinds of people. Most of all, infants reduce all questions to the very basic one of life and death. The infant Jesus puts God at that radical moment. In such natural surroundings as the birth of a child, God suddenly appears, as abruptly as the prophet Elijah.

Yet as Jesus and John the Baptist proceeded in their work, they encountered ever more opposition. Because John the Baptist confronted Herod the Tetrarch for his immoral union with his brother's wife, he was eventually beheaded. Because Jesus strove to bring dignity to people considered "outlaws" by religious authorities he too began to be hounded by opposition and even open persecution. Both John the Baptist and Jesus stood up for common decency and normal human dignity.

They worked for unity, but we notice that it was not unity at any cost. This new bond between brothers and sisters had to manifest honor and purity of heart, kindliness and forgiveness. These virtues seem so easy to recognize, so crucial as to render all discussion unnecessary. This honorable way of life seems possible by following a few simple instructions.

Yet, how much we all resist these easy solutions. The unity which Jesus seeks, expects us to form one family of love, yet we will continue to hold on to grudges, hurts and bad memories. To continue with such enmity and division brings us ever closer to great tragedies, like the crucifixion of Jesus. A family member may die without reconciliation and we must continue living with great regret and a conscience that punishes us severely.

Jesus came to save us from such wrath.

Prayer:

Lord Jesus, come quickly! Stir up our longings for peace and reconciliation. Grant us the strength to forgive and forget, so that we can bring our finest gifts of charity to form a reunion worthy of your spirit.

Monday, Third Week of Advent*

Num 24:2–7,15–17. Balaam saw a vision of an oasis-like paradise and of a star rising from Israel.

Matt 21:23–27. Because the religious leaders refused to commit themselves about John the Baptist, Jesus would not tell them by what authority he spoke and acted.

We must be honest with ourselves, with others and with God who is over all. We cannot forever dodge questions, camouflage the truth, and bluff our way along. In the case of Balaam, a foreign prophet was hired by Balak, king of Moab, to curse Israel. Yet the messengers of the king could not induce him to act against the Lord's will. Balaam replied:

> Even if Balak gave me his house full of silver and gold, I could not do anything, small or great, contrary to the command of the Lord, my God. But, you too [like the earlier messengers] shall stay here overnight, till I learn what else the Lord may tell me (Num 22:18–19).

From the last sentence we see that Balaam was anxious to be given an oracle from the Lord agreeable to the king. "Stay overnight," he says, maybe tomorrow I will learn something else from the Lord! The story takes on a touch of humor at this point. Because Balaam was toying with the hope that the Lord might eventually change the

---

*For the Masses from December 17 to 24, turn to the meditation immediately following Friday of this week.

message to one congenial to the Moabite King, the donkey on which he was riding became stubborn, went off the road and even talked back to Balaam. When Balaam attempted to beat the donkey into submission, the animal said: "Am I not your own beast, and have you not always ridden upon me until now?" The implication is: animals are more obedient than human beings. The prophet Isaiah used the same example effectively:

> An ox knows its owner,
>> and an ass, its master's manger;
> But Israel does not know,
>> my people has not understood.
>
> (Is 1:3)

Where animals respond directly and continually, people will go in circles to deny or avoid the obvious. In the last resort they will simply refuse to answer. Such was the case of the religious leaders in Jesus' day. When they challenged Jesus' authority to heal and to teach, Jesus replied:

> I too will ask a question [of you]. If you answer it for me, then I will tell you on what authority I do the things I do. What was the origin of John's baptism? Was it divine or merely human?

The leaders feared the people's wrath to infer that John the Baptist was a fake. Yet under no conditions were they willing to agree that John who pointed to Jesus as the promised one could ever have spoken with divine authority. So their reply to Jesus was: "We do not know."

If people from all ways of life persistently called

John a prophet and remained loyal to him even when it was politically dangerous because of Herod the Tetrarch, then the odds are highly in favor of John that he was a genuine prophet and spoke with divine authority. Common sense and a strong consensus among many good people cannot be denied without denying God, their creator, nor can anyone remain passive or neutral when such a person as John speaks in the name of God.

Both biblical readings, in a sense, reach deeply into the flesh and blood of human life as created by God. A pagan prophet, despite his greedy desire for royal gifts, cannot resist the compelling inspiration of the people whom God has led out of Egypt. They possessed a strength, a forward vision, a consecration, an integral goodness which promised a future when "a star shall advance from Jacob." John the Baptist preached the solid virtues of honesty, generosity, hope, humility, loyalty. In Luke 3:11–16, John declared:

> [To] the person with two coats give to him who
> has none.
> Tax collectors, exact nothing over and above your
> fixed amount.
> Soldiers, do not bully anyone. Denounce no one
> falsely.
> One is to come [after me] mightier than I.
> I am not fit to loosen his sandal strap.

Finally, he was imprisoned and eventually executed for denouncing Herod the Tetrarch for incest with his brother's wife (Matt 14:3).

Sophisticated people of academia or religion—all of us in areas of life where we are educated and secure—will continually be challenged by common folk who speak the honest-to-God truth. Unless we listen to them and reply humbly Jesus will say to us: "Neither will I tell you on what authority I do the things I do."

Prayer:

Lord, give me an open heart to listen and a willing spirit to respond. Your prophets, Jeremiah and Isaiah, announced that people will come from the ends of the earth, to acclaim the Savior's presence. Help me listen to these new and surprising voices that teach me your ways, O Lord.

Tuesday, Third Week of Advent

Zeph 3:1–2,9–13. The people of Israel who once refused correction will be cleansed; as God's remnant they "need not be ashamed" anymore of their misdeeds.

Matt 21:28–32. Those who speak and look pious yet secretly do not follow the will of the Lord will not enter the kingdom of God while tax collectors and prostitutes who appear evil yet repent of their sins will be invited in.

It seems that one of the most difficult impressions to cast off is a sense of shame. People will never allow tax collectors and prostitutes—the male and female occupations, considered to be the most shameful in Palestine during the days of Jesus—ever to forget that they were tax collectors and prostitutes. Once upon a time, in the days of the prophet Zephaniah, all Israel was reduced to such a condition. The prophet cried out:

Woe to the city, rebellious and polluted,
    to the tyrannical city!

She hears no voice,
    accepts no correction.

The prophet, nonetheless, projected a vision of hope. Foreign nations would call upon the name of the Lord, and Israel was consoled with these words:

You need not be ashamed of all your deeds,
    your rebellious actions against me. . . .
I will leave as a remnant in your midst
    a people humble and lowly.

God can remove shame and bring his people back to the dignity of their first creation. This transformation will happen at a time when foreign nations will "call upon the name of the Lord, to serve him with one accord." The removal of shame, such a monumental task that human beings seldom if ever allow it to happen, takes place in a world setting. The prophet implies that the necessary ingredients for this change do not come from sophisticated knowledge of the Mosaic law nor from careful following of the temple rubrics. In fact, Israel had been taking pride in her legal and ceremonial behavior. She felt so confident that "she hears no voice, accepts no correction."

The prophet reaches beneath religion to the deep, natural level of human existence, where men and women exist simply as God's creatures. Every person begins in the womb of his mother simply as God's creature. Flesh and blood we share with everyone else whether this other person is religious or not. Our human nature with its common sense and common decency asks that shame be removed.

This newly found human dignity also implies what is again one of the basic qualities of God's creation. As infants we are "a people humble and lowly," and such smallness and poverty attract God's tender delight and strong compassion. He says about this lowly remnant:

> They shall do no wrong
>   and speak no lies;
> Nor shall there be found in their mouths
>   a deceitful tongue.

God's humble remnant possesses the simple honesty and extraordinary human dignity of the child.

Zephaniah's words were not easily composed; they must have provoked a disagreeable reception among the people. He implied the destruction of Jerusalem, the conversion of the invading foreigners, the humble rather than triumphal revival of the people. The transition from shame to human dignity exerts a heavy cost.

Jesus faced up to this demanding ministry of reconciling tax collectors and prostitutes, shameful people if there ever were any in the estimation of religious authority at that time. To do so, he gave a simple example of a man with two sons. The first son put on a pious appearance and always said and did the right thing, or at least made people think that he did! The comparison with religious and civil authorities was far too evident to need further elaboration. The other son was mischievous, disobedient, saucy, self-willed; he always replied first with a quick "No!" before he had time to think. He was like the tax collectors and the prostitutes who made no show of religion at all. And yet they silently repented and humbly listened to John the Baptist. John spoke to them as people whose shame could be lifted and whose human dignity still resided within them and could be revived.

These people quietly changed their life, humbly returned to God, determined to "do no wrong and speak no lies," as the prophet Zephaniah advised. Yet the religious people never wanted this shame to be lifted nor their former profession to be forgotten.

Jesus asks the question of us: do we allow people to regain their human dignity or do we continually bring up their shameful past? Jesus, born as an infant, recalls our basic human quality as created by God. This simple fact not only cries out for tenderness and honesty but also for the mercy by which we give each person a chance to be truly who he is, as innocent as God's creation will always be.

Let us make no pretense about it. To pass from shame to human dignity will never be easy. We will suffer the same slur as did Jesus, "a friend of tax collectors and prostitutes." Jesus took the words as a compliment, but suffered for it. We will suffer too by simply allowing people, once sinful, again to be converted to their human goodness, to be our friends and to "call upon the name of the Lord."

Prayer:

Lord, you hear the cry of the poor, so that the lowly are made glad and radiant with joy. No longer will their faces blush with shame. Lord, enable me also to hear the same cry of the poor, to be one with them and radiant with their joy. Then my shame too will be taken away.

Wednesday, Third Week of Advent

Is 45:6–8,18,21–25. I, the Lord, create light and darkness, send forth salvation like dew from heaven, and
reestablish the earth for my people, so that everyone
shall swear, "Only in the Lord are just deeds and power."

Luke 7:18–23. John the Baptist sent two disciples to Jesus, asking, "Are you 'he who is to come'?" Jesus answered by curing the blind and the lame and thus
bringing good news to the poor.

According to the prophet Isaiah, the Lord creates
both light and darkness, well-being and woe. These contrary forces of human existence meet in another way in
the Gospel. John the Baptist, already imprisoned by Herod the Tetrarch (Matt 11:2) and surrounded by darkness
and woe, sends messengers to Jesus. The question put to
Jesus reveals further darkness and quandary in John the
Baptist, "Are you 'He who is come' or are we to expect
someone else?" Jesus replied in a burst of energy and sun-
light:

> Go and report to John ... The blind recover
> their sight, cripples walk, lepers are cured, the
> deaf hear, dead people are raised to life, and the
> poor have the good news preached to them.

John the Baptist was reassured that Jesus is the promised
one by extraordinary works of compassion. Yet these
marvelous acts of deliverance were denied to John the
Baptist who was left in prison, soon to be executed because of the scheming revenge of Herodias and the weakness of the Tetrarch.

Today's Scripture places clearly before us the biblical expectation of faith: we are to believe that Jesus is the Lord of both life and death, of both light and darkness, of both strength and weakness. Both phenomena require a strong faith. We can be swept away by joy and prosperity and totally forget the presence of God. We can be embittered by pain and disappointment and rebel against God. If we are sick, we must believe that Jesus can cure us, even though he deliberately decides not to do so, just as he left John the Baptist in prison. If we are in good health, we must believe that it is God's gift to be shared and expended for others.

In both cases we are faced with a *mystery* of faith. As such, no amount of reasoning can explain why God creates and directs darkness and woe equally as much as he forms light and well-being. We can investigate the universe without finding an adequate clue to this mystery. At such a time we find out how impossible it is for us to comprehend God's decisions. The same prophet of the Babylonian exile who wrote today's first reading almost ridicules those people who pretend to advise God and understand his ways. He asks them to use their human means of measuring the universe. It is impossible:

> Who [among you] has cupped in his hand the
>   waters of the sea,
>   and marked off the heavens with a span?
> Who has held in a measure the dust of the earth,
>   weighed the mountains in scales and the hills
>   in a balance?

The obvious answer, of course, is "No one!" Then the prophet puts the key question:

Who has directed the spirit of the Lord,
   or has instructed him as his counselor?

Faced with mystery, the prophet took his question back before the moment of creation. In other words God *must* have an answer, so sublime that no one of us can comprehend it. Each moment of our lives has a definite place within God's creation. The moments of darkness and woe are as important as the cycle of day and night, night and day, for good ecological balance.

This cycle ought to be present in all of our community enterprises and neighborhood meetings. We ought to manifest both strength and weakness, strong decisions and humble dependence. With this combination, we will complement one another and sustain one another; we will arrive at the wisest decision available at the time. And in our reaction toward others, we will reveal ourselves as a people, already in possession of salvation by our strengths and talents, much in need of salvation by our faults and weaknesses. We will be instructors of others and will be instructed by these same persons. Then the earth will open and salvation bud forth!

Prayer:
   Let the clouds rain down the Just One and the earth bring forth a savior. You, Lord Jesus, are as immediately present as rain and flowers, or you vanish like a bird across the sky. For as Job asked, who knows the storehouse of the snow, who has begotten rain and the drops of dew? In the wonder of what is closest to me, enable me to live with the mystery of yourself far beyond me.

Thursday, Third Week of Advent

Is 54:1–10. Once a wife barren and forsaken, Israel is called back to the Lord. "Your maker is your husband."

Luke 7:24–30. The entire populace was attracted to John the Baptist, the prophet commissioned to prepare the way of the Lord. Only the official religious leaders refused to be baptized by John and to be put in readiness for the Messiah.

What monumental efforts God sets in motion in order to come to us and to attract us to himself. At times, as in Isaiah, God's word is heard in tones of intimate love. At other times as in the reading from Luke, God speaks through a stern and uncompromising prophet like John the Baptist. If we are to find God, we must allow ourselves to be found by him. By faith we recognize that God speaks in a way corresponding to our needs and personality: at times with severity, at other times with tenderness. We must guard against the disposition of many of the Pharisees and lawyers who could not tolerate the swift, clean way by which John the Baptist cut through religious formality to basic human needs and expectations. We need to meditate on these various ways of God, so that our own response will be quick, obedient and effective.

God can come to us in tender, affectionate ways. The selection from Isaiah consists of a long poem whose each new stanza ends with a crescendo of divine love: says the Lord, says *your* God, says the Lord *your Redeemer,* says the Lord *who has mercy on you.* The simple yet majestic title of Yahweh or Lord, Israel's specially revealed name for God, becomes all the more a part of Israel's life in the phrase, *your* God. The author of this poem, usually called Second Isaiah (see the meditation for Tuesday, Second Week of Advent) seldom uses the generic word "God," but almost always draws God into the circle of Israel's family. The next title, *Lord your Redeemer,* unites Yahweh within Israel's blood relationship; the Hebrew word for Redeemer means kin or relative and the consequent obligations, as in Lev 25:24,30,36,41. United by blood, the Lord is one *who has mercy on you,* as we read in the final line of the poem, yet in a most intimate way. "Mercy" here is drawn from a word in the Hebrew language, meaning "womb." God's love surrounds us as a child in its mother's womb.

God, on the contrary, at times will not treat us delicately as an unborn infant but sternly as a responsible adult. Such was certainly the case when he spoke through his prophet John the Baptist. John was a no-person. He lived in the desert wilderness of Judah, was clothed in camel's hair and leather belt, ate grasshoppers and wild honey (Mark 1:6) and cried out:

> You brood of vipers! Who told you to flee from the wrath to come? Give some evidence that you mean to reform. . . . Every tree that is not fruitful will be cut down and thrown into the fire (Luke 3:7–9).

John cut through rank, privilege and wealth and proposed a common sense morality of basic right and wrong, uncompromised by moral casuistry or religious sophistication.

In a few quick strokes, Jesus drew John's portrait:

> What did you go out to see in the desert?—a reed swayed by the wind? . . . someone dressed

luxuriously eating in splendor? . . . a prophet?
He is that, I assure you, and something more.

According to the blunt talk of John the Baptist, we
accept God on God's terms. From today's biblical readings we realize that God can speak tenderly . . . or harshly! It is a fearful and scary moment when we allow God
the liberty of approaching us in any way that God judges
best for us. He may reach out to us tenderly or severely.
His "Advent" may involve a long preparation, the way
that Second Isaiah drew upon centuries' old traditions
and carefully composed an elaborate, doctrinal poem. Or
God may burst upon us like those prophets who come
into our lives without even a conventional how-do-you-
do? In this latter case we think of the sudden appearance
of Elijah in 1 Kings 17 or of John the Baptist particularly
in Mark 1:1–4,

> Here begins the Gospel of Jesus Christ, the Son
> of God. In Isaiah the prophet it is written, "I
> send my messenger before you . . ." Thus it was
> that John the Baptist appeared.

God may act "democratically" or "philosophically"
and permit us a stretch of time to think it over. Or God
may demand an immediate "Yes!"

In the latter case we cannot protest, "But God, did
you not give us a mind for thinking it over?" In the former case, however, we are obliged to meditate through
many hours of silence.

Sometimes we complain that we cannot find God.
Maybe it would be more accurate to state: we are not allowing ourselves to be found by God! This idea lies behind St. Paul's insistence that "the just person shall live

by faith" and not by works (Rom 1:17; 4:1–5). At crucial
moments God reaches beneath all human works and expects an immediate, even a blind "Yes, I believe." These
moments are not reduced to a single method, for God
speaks "in fragmentary and various ways" (Heb 1:1).
This phrase comes from the Epistle to the Hebrews
which later in Chapter 11 tells of the *many, diverse* ways
by which God summons a response of faith.

Prayer:
    Lord, enable me this Advent to prepare for your
coming by a deeper attitude of faith, so that I find you
very near in each and every moment of my life, very near
in each person or event that crosses the path of my life.

Friday, Third Week of Advent

Is 56:1–3,6–8. My house shall be a house of prayer for all
    peoples, who harbor a spirit of hope and keep their
    hand from evildoing.
John 5:33–36. John the Baptist was a light, testifying to
    Jesus, and now Jesus' own works give testimony that
    the Father has sent him.

    Today's biblical passages face up to a phenomenon
very difficult for most of us to handle. Put simply, the
problem is this: what we ourselves spend a long time to
acquire, others accomplish quickly. Hidden within this
human situation is the complementary fact that in a different set of circumstances we are fast and others are
slow. Yet the humiliating pain still strikes us, and we

question God: "Why must I labor so long and hard for what others obtain so easily and so simply?"

Within the first century of Christianity it was hard for the Jewish Christians to see gentiles acquiring full status within the Church without submitting to the long, disciplinary and doctrinal preparation of the Jewish law and Scriptures. Not even Jesus dispensed with this preparation, and all of those whom he chose as "prophets and apostles" to be the foundations of the Church (Eph 2:20) were thoroughly Jewish in their formation and piety. Even Paul, who declared almost belligerently, "neither circumcision nor the lack of it counts for anything, only faith," also wrote in the same epistle to the Galatians: "I made progress in Jewish observance far beyond most of my contemporaries" (Gal 5:6; 1:14). If Paul discounted Jewish practices as unnecessary, his Jewish adversaries could say, "Yes, that is true, only because you have learned and followed them so faithfully!"

We can turn to everyday occurrences for some advice and direction. Doctors and lawyers study long years about good health and sound legal practice, while many other people maintain their health instinctively by good simple habits of eating, sleeping and relaxing, and they remain at peace with the law by a normal routine at work and at home. Yet, doctors and lawyers do not begrudge these people their health and peace! Other cases are not as easily settled. Some women can bear children with relative ease, while others pass through an ordeal of physical agony and/or mental depression with each pregnancy. There is bound to be some angry jealousy on one side and some questioning impatience on the other.

Doctors and lawyers are at no disadvantage for long grueling years of study about medicine and law; parents are not being penalized when asked by God to suffer more for the sake of their children. Always, whatever costs more is appreciated more. At least this is the case if we are normal human beings.

If Israel has endured more agony than almost any other nation in recorded history, Israel ought not to be upset if the gentiles come into the kingdom quickly. Not only will God always remember the loyalty of his people, but they will possess within their family traditions a strength, a devotion, a sense of true values far more precious than money can purchase. Israel's pre-disposition for faith far exceeds the attitude of most other people. Just as a long family tradition of farming or handicrafts or banking imparts an ancestral wisdom which could come only with time, likewise as St. Paul wrote, Israel, the true olive branch, can much more easily be grafted onto the root of an olive tree than we gentiles whom the apostle calls wild olive branches (Rom 11:13–24).

Yet every family with ancestral wisdom needs new blood, new ideas and new challenge. Likewise Israel was to be enriched by the ingrafting of gentiles within the true olive tree. Whatever we possess, is not worth possessing unless it is shared with others and thereby enriched. As Jesus said: whoever loses their life for the sake of the Kingdom of God, saves it; and whoever saves their life selfishly and fearfully, loses it to mediocrity and eventually to silent extinction (Luke 9:24).

For our part then we treasure the gift of faith, handed down to us from our ancestors' suffering and perseverance. We also treasure each opportunity to freely and quickly share this gift with others. Outsiders will bring their own centuries' old traditions to enrich us in our ancestral faith. Finally let us glory in the fact that our children and descendants may far surpass us as Jesus advanced far beyond John the Baptist. Jesus said:

I have testimony greater than John's,
namely, the works the Father has given me to
accomplish.

Prayer:
Lord, grant that what I have suffered to achieve, I may share freely with others. Give me the noble gift of silent generosity. I trust that this silence will be rewarded by strength and peace like yours, Lord Jesus, born humbly at Bethlehem.

December 17

Gen 49:2,8–10. In the liturgical blessing upon the twelve tribes, Judah receives the promise of royalty.
Matt 1:1–17. The genealogy of Jesus was of the line of Judah through Joseph his foster-father.

Centuries of politics and intrigue, of theological hopes and purifying sufferings, of exegetical problems and serious questions of biblical interpretation converge upon us in today's biblical reading. Without attempting to solve these difficulties nor even to isolate and clarify what they are, our own religious reflections will rebound from various aspects of the political and literary history of the royal life of Judah and the family of David.

Moses had not legislated for kings. He had invested authority in priests, elders and tribal leaders. Only a serious threat to Israel's survival, two centuries after Moses, forced such a radical change as the institution of a royal dynasty. The blessings upon the tribes in Genesis Chapter 49 represent an important step in this transition. While the tribal blessings in Deuteronomy Chapter 33

say very little about Judah, Genesis Chapter 49 openly
endorses the royal privileges of Judah, either to silence opposition against the innovation of kingship or to celebrate
its advantages for Israel. The pro- and anti-monarchic
traditions in 1 Samuel Chapters 8–10 offer a limited view
of the same struggle over royalty.

The infancy narrative in Luke's and Matthew's gospels shows the struggle of the early Church to establish
the origins and privileges of Jesus and his family. Matthew's gospel will sweep into a worldwide posture. The
genealogy implies an involvement in world politics like
the Babylonian exile, foreign ancestors like Tamar and
Ruth, and the established plan of God within three series
of fourteen generations. It is clear that the brilliant empires of David and Solomon did not fulfill God's plans.
Therefore, the Church must set up God's universal kingdom.

Yet, our reflections are caught in a serious theological question. In the days of David and up to the Babylonian empire, everyone took for granted that the eternal
promises to David in 2 Samuel 7 meant what they said,
that an offspring of the Davidic line would always be en-
throned as king of Judah and Israel. And when the dynasty was humiliated or even deprived of all royal
privileges, the people could only question and remon-
strate with God and ask "How long?" as we read in the
final verses of Psalm 89.

God's promises were fulfilled in David, but they
were not exhausted by David. Here is where we are faced
with serious consequences. Our understanding of the
Scriptures may be correct but never exhaustive. God can
hold many surprises in store for us. What we may grasp
so wonderfully and so jealously as the fulfillment of
God's word in our own lives or in the Church of our day,

may mirror only a small part of what God intends for us in that word.

In order for the next stage of fulfillment to be realized, we may have to suffer our "Babylonian exile," the loss of our best gifts, and the question will be forced from us, "How long, Lord?" God's answer this Advent is: till a child is born. There are no quick, military solutions to God's promises. What David and Solomon achieved were inspired by God and blessed again and again by the Lord in the temple ritual. Yet, God was preparing for a fulfillment far more stupendous, a world kingdom of lowliness and poverty. Then it will be all the more apparent that *God* is king. God therefore will challenge all of our quick solutions and forced applications—in the birth of a child. "Unless you become . . . like little children, you will not enter the kingdom of God" (Matt 18:3).

Matthew's gospel records foreign women like Tamar, Ruth, and Bathsheba, all of whom bear a blight upon their character. Tamar dressed as a sacred or temple prostitute to win Judah's favor and conceive a child through him! Ruth entered biblical history as a polytheist! Bathsheba seduced David and began a series of assassinations within the royal family (2 Sam 11–20). The fourth woman to be named in this genealogy is Mary, who acquired royal privileges only through her husband Joseph. Jesus, therefore, inherited the Davidic promises by a legal fiction: through his foster father Joseph.

We too will come to dwell in the house of God's promises only by kindly receiving strangers and foreigners, even people with little or no reputation. We will be at home only by opening the doors of our homes to foreigners. If we are selfish or indifferent, fearful or distant, we will lose what little we possess and be driven away from the ancestral line of God's promises. Strangers usually come unannounced into our lives. Yet here too we must be prepared to recognize a careful plan of God, to fulfill that exact number of fourteen generations, thrice repeated.

God's surprises are carefully within the divine plan; our understanding of that plan will be tested by unanticipated turns of events. People too may startle us by their words and actions. Is our heart open to them? Only if it is, will Joseph bring his wife, pregnant with child, into our heart and home.

Prayer:

Lord, Wisdom of God Most High, teach me to walk in your paths and to open my heart and home to each and every stranger. Then the heavens will sing for joy and the earth exult. Our Lord Jesus is coming who takes pity on us in our distress.

December 18

Jer 23:5–8. God will raise up a righteous shoot from the root of David and its name shall be "The Lord our Justice." God's people will be reassembled in their own land.

Matt 1:18–24. Joseph accepts Mary as his wife, even though the child which she is carrying is not his own but "by the Holy Spirit." And so the words of the prophet Isaiah are fulfilled.

Advent is a time of fulfillment and of surprises. We become all the more convinced that the Lord will live up to all his promises in the Scriptures and to all the hopes in human hearts. God, therefore, is given the name, "The

Lord our Justice—*Yahweh Sidqenu.*" He justly, in fact abundantly accomplishes his word and his hopes.

At first, however, it must have seemed to the prophets Isaiah and Jeremiah that the Lord's oracles were being annulled and profaned, not sanctified and accomplished. Each witnessed the deterioration of the Davidic dynasty. Kings who occupied the throne were apostates like King Ahaz (2 Kgs 16) or weaklings like King Zedekiah (Jer 38:5,19,24–26). Even if God were to be faithful to his promises to David of an everlasting dynasty (2 Sam 7:16), it was a disservice to support a corrupt royal house. The whole situation seemed to be a no-win predicament for the Lord.

Joseph, too, newly engaged to Mary, was also faced with a baffling and painful enigma. He could not accept the obvious implication that Mary had already been unfaithful to him, even before their marriage, and he could not deny the obvious fact that Mary was pregnant. He was forced to take a human course of action and divorce Mary quietly. Soon afterward, he was willing to accept the revelation of an angel that Mary had conceived this child by the overshadowing of the Holy Spirit.

Here is a strange combination of supernaturally "hoping against hope" (Rom 4:18) that Mary was innocent and of following a natural decision that was kind but resolute, a quiet divorce. Joseph is to be admired all the more when he again reversed himself. After arriving at a conclusion which cost him hours and days of excruciating agony and soul-searching puzzlement, he followed the angel's advice and accepted Mary into his home as his wife. Then he followed the secret resolution: though loving her tenderly he resolved never to have marital relations with Mary.

The prophets Isaiah and Jeremiah, when confronted

with an impossible set of circumstances, also combined an unconditional and even a blind attitude of faith with human keenness and cautious concern. Because the dynasty had degenerated so badly that God's divinely endowed king was worshiping other gods and was rejecting the Lord's word through his prophets, the house or tree of David must be cut down so that nothing remained but a stump above ground or maybe just a root hidden within the earth. While this human solution seemed blasphemous enough to deny God's everlasting promises to David, there was still a remnant of divine hope. Someday, someway, the spirit would rest upon this root or stump (Is 11:1) and so God would "raise up a righteous shoot."

This prophecy was fulfilled in ways that reached far beyond the imagination of Isaiah and Jeremiah. Yet, the fulfillment lay within a straight line of development. The prophets were declaring that the dynasty would revive in such a way that everyone would know that "God is just." Therefore, God's name must be *"Yahweh Sidqenu."*

We too can be faced with puzzling and agonizing situations which seem to deny God's goodness and justice. God never asks us to betray our human intelligence. God gave us a mind and a store of ancestral wisdom by which to form prudent decisions. Yet, within this human process God will intervene at times and overwhelm us with the miraculous. We feel like Mary the virgin who is with child. Without doing anything or with a sweep of wonder reaching far beyond our human activity, God will act. We can only exclaim "Immanuel—God is with us." We will call God "Yahweh Sidqenu," for he is justly fulfilling his promises and our hopes far beyond all expectation. The fulfillment will be like a tender shoot, growing from a hidden root. What is so miraculous, must be surrounded with the most tender human care.

Prayer:

Come, Lord, Leader of ancient Israel! Enable us to keep faith in our human nature, your creation, our responsibility. Yet, as we think, reflect and seek advice, keep us always open to your wondrous intervention, your *Immanuel.*

December 19

Judg 13:2–7, 24–25. The conception of Samson is announced to a woman barren for a long time. The child is to be consecrated to the Lord as a Nazirite for his entire lifetime.

Luke 1:5–25. The conception of John the Baptist is announced to Zechariah, who doubts because of the couple's old age. His wife Elizabeth does conceive this child who is to remain a Nazirite till his death.

Advent is a continuous reminder that God will work miracles to bring his promises and our worthy hopes to completion. Advent also proclaims its faith in human nature. God acts miraculously within the sequence of normal human activity! Even when the situation seems hopeless, we must never forsake hope but continue along our day-by-day line of duties, confident in God and in our human existence.

In today's readings two barren couples must have taken it for granted that they would have no children of their own. Having accepted the situation, they must have arranged all the other details of their marriage accordingly. Their home and income, their work and relaxation, their mental attitudes and verbal responses, everything about their person and their relationship with others had been adjusted.

How difficult it must be to revive hopes for a child. They must have reasoned together that they cannot endure facing such possibilities, only to be let down again with frustration. It is far easier to take for granted that they are not meant to have their own children. How many ups and downs can a marriage tolerate?

Evidently for Zechariah it was too much. He would not go lightly through such a travail of hope, only to be frustrated and let down—unless the angel produced a solid reason and a supernatural sign. Samson's future mother was far more easily induced to believe, to hope and to try.

Zechariah was to be made all the more dependent. He was struck speechless and was to remain that way till after the birth of the child. We might even find a mystical meaning here: no human words can possibly communicate the mystery of what God could do.

Each child, Samson and John, was consecrated as a Nazirite at its birth, according to the rules set down in Numbers 6:1–21. In many ways the order or institution of Nazirites symbolized the wondrous exploits of the early Mosaic days. It caught the force of the "Holy Wars," when survival for Israel in the desert evoked all the mightiest forces of human existence. Moses, too, projected the image of a leader who summoned people against all natural odds to march forward and to take possession of their promised land. They were God's warriors, God was their leader (Ex 15). The Nazirite's hair was uncut; we all recall Absalom's long hair at a time of war (2 Sam 18:9). They could not touch any liquor, for strong drink was especially devastating among desert nomads. Nazirites then symbolized those fierce days when everyone belonged totally to God and roused hidden strength through absolute obedience to the Lord's will.

Each of us needs the symbol of the Nazirite vow within our daily existence. We are helped immensely by some sign which says to us: how wonderfully, even how miraculously God has cared for you. Out of concern for others each of us should convey some sign to others of our intense faith in God who at times will work miracles for our sake. This "Nazirite vow" can take many forms. We think of the widow who placed a single shekel in the temple treasury, yet in doing so she dug into her dire poverty and rendered herself all the more destitute and helpless (Luke 21:1–4). Or the "Nazirite Vow" may show up in the way by which we go the extra mile (Matt 5:41). When we think to have done more than enough and expended our energy already too much, God says, once more I ask you for this favor! In other words we must be heroic at certain moments of our lives and we need to remember these moments as a continuous sign of our total dedication to the Lord.

Prayer:

Come, Lord Jesus, flower of Jesse's stem, wondrous child where life seemed dead. Come, revive my life and my faith in your miraculous presence. Make me a sign, your Nazirite, of how we ought to live totally for you.

December 20

Is 7:10–14. The birth of Immanuel is a sign that God will
    save his people in miraculous ways.
Luke 1:26–38. The angel Gabriel announced to Mary
    that she is to be the mother of the Savior-Messiah.

God's plan for world salvation reaches a climax and
fulfillment in the conception of Jesus. Conceived within
the womb of Mary, Jesus was as fully human as anyone
of us. Just as God had obeyed the laws of human history
through Old Testament times, he would bring the process
of redemption to its final stage in the incarnation of the
Word, the second person of the Holy Trinity. Luke is
fully conscious of this historical, human setting, not only
by linking the birth of Jesus with the census of Quirinius
(Luke 2:1–2) but also by introducing the public ministry
of Jesus with a long historical prologue (Luke 3:1–2).
This interaction with the politics and geography of human existence is also recognized in our Creed: "suffered
under Pontius Pilate."
    If a person takes the time to read the opening verses
1–9 before today's selection from Isaiah, he will find the
political involvement of the prophet with the king during
the crisis of the Syro-Ephraimite League. Two northern
kingdoms—Syria with its capital at Damascus and
Ephraim or Israel with its capital at Samaria—were on
the verge of invading the southern kingdom of Judah. Jerusalem was in a panic and the king had already decided
on his course of action. He would declare his country a
vassal of Assyria, pay the heavy tribute and so save his
throne. King Ahaz was all the more fearful because his
royal line at this moment could be blotted out. His only
son had already been sacrificed to the god Moloch (2
Kings 16:3).

Isaiah's answer was as simple as it was difficult—do nothing but trust in God. Your dynasty will survive. The Syro-Ephraimite league will collapse without selling the independence of the country to Assyria. With a false show of religious piety, Ahaz replied: "I will not tempt the Lord!"

Isaiah then announced the birth of Immanuel, a symbolic name given to the child which Ahaz' new wife was about to conceive. Isaiah insists that this child will inherit the throne not through Ahaz' political maneuvering but solely by the Lord's direction. Assyria will turn upon Judah and cruelly invade the country (Is 8:5–8). Yet when the power to which Ahaz appealed for protection becomes an instrument of destruction, God will exert a subtle yet all-powerful influence which reaches beyond human calculations and human ability. The bottom line declared very clearly: God alone saves!

This message of Isaiah found a new and surprising development with the conception of Jesus. Like any other child, Jesus would come to birth after nine months within his mother's womb. Jesus would be born in a family setting of a man and woman married as husband and wife. Jesus, therefore, did not suddenly appear as an adult on one of the mountains of Judah: he did not come abruptly from a distant place like the prophet Elijah (1 Kings 17:1). Jesus not only was born after nine months of pregnancy but he also spent long silent years at Nazareth as infant, boy and young man. This stretch of time has no value for world salvation except that Jesus the Messiah would be thoroughly human.

The normal human laws or customs of marriage reached into the home where Jesus grew up. As husband and wife, Joseph and Mary loved each other dearly. Their attitude toward one another—their way of looking and exchanging glances of special love, their way of entertaining friends and of discussing their home, their work and the child's education—all this imparted the impression of an ideal married couple.

Yet, again as in the case of human history in the days of Isaiah, God intervened in ways that took everyone by surprise; at least Mary and Joseph were startled. Jesus would be miraculously conceived and throughout their marriage Joseph would respect Mary's virginal consecration. Mary's virginal conception of Jesus and virginal relationship with Joseph are in no way a norm for a happy marriage in the lives of other couples. Yet there is a symbol or type here that must be verified in everyone's life.

The angel Gabriel's announcement to Mary of her virginal conception of Jesus, the Savior, symbolizes how God will surely step into all of our lives, right when we are midstream in the course of our human existence, right at crucial moments of our planning. The way of salvation will take a sudden turn, our plans must be scuttled, and what we had never suspected to happen, becomes the principal element in our lives. Only by interacting positively with this sudden divine intervention— perhaps a serious sickness or death, a financial loss, a new child within the family, a new in-law—very natural in some ways yet totally unexpected in most ways—can we find peace and salvation. Looking back, we will confess: only God saves.

Prayer:

Come, Lord Jesus, Key of David. Open the gates of fear so that we walk with faith and willingly accept the surprising turns of your holy will. Mary, Mother of faith, intercede for us that we follow your example.

December 21

Song of Songs 2:8–14. My lover speaks: "Arise, my beautiful one. The winter is past."
Zeph 3:14–18.* The prophet's song of deliverance summons Jerusalem to rejoice, for "the Lord . . . is in your midst" and is rejoicing over you with gladness."
Luke 1:39–45. Mary visits her cousin Elizabeth who also is with child.

Both the Song of Songs and the prophet Zephaniah announce the end of a difficult period. The lover says to his bride in the Song of Songs:

> For see, the winter is past,
>   the rains are over and gone.
> The flowers appear on the earth.

Zephaniah is generally considered a book of gloom, and some of its darkness remains in the passage of today's Mass:

> The Lord has removed the judgment against you,
>   [O Zion]
> you have no further misfortune to fear.

In the Gospel the sad barren period of Elizabeth's life has been abruptly ended by her conception of John the Baptist.

We too need this divine assurance that every sorrow and tragedy must end. These difficulties cannot continue forever. The pattern occurs repeatedly in the Bible. In

* Alternate first reading.

fact the last book of the New Testament, called Revelation, states unequivocally in its second to last chapter:

> God shall wipe every tear from their eyes, and
> there shall be no more death or mourning, cry-
> ing out or pain, for the former world has passed
> away (Rev 21:4).

Even when it ends, sorrow still remains a mystery for us. We cannot help asking of God: if you love us as tenderly as the Song of Songs declares so melodiously, then why did you tolerate so much hardship in our lives? Can you say to us:

> Your voice is sweet,
> and you are lovely,

and all the while wrap our minds in worry, our hearts in disappointment, our bodies in pain?

Just as the fact of pain remains a mystery, neither can we determine ahead of time the kind of joy which will be ours. This too is God's secret. This fact becomes very clear in Elizabeth's exclamation to Mary:

> Blessed is *she who trusted* that the Lord's
> words to her would be fulfilled.

Some joys and triumphs are very difficult to handle! Suppose that we inherit a castle. Most of us would not know what to do with it but sell it! The deepest or most fragile joy comes to us in people. Each new friend and especially each new member of a family places very heavy responsibilities upon us at the same time that they bring delicate satisfaction and tender hopes.

Today's Scriptures celebrate the joy of pregnancy with Mary and Elizabeth and center their hopes around Jesus and John the Baptist. The Song of Songs and even more clearly the prophet Zephaniah call upon Jerusalem/Zion to shout for joy over the birth of the promised children. Yet we all know very well what sorrow would come to Mary and Elizabeth because of their children and what tragedy would envelop Jerusalem because of Jesus.

Both sorrow and joy are wrapped in mystery. Somehow or other our weeping ought not to be so loud as to drown the sweet songs of joy; our happiness ought never to distract us from our suffering brothers and sisters. In this way we will be prepared for the cycle of sadness and happiness which will occur over and over until God finally wipes away every tear. Individually and as a family, we pass our lives in a delicate interchange of joy and sorrow. Each is lost in the mystery of God's love.

We asked: How can God who loves us tenderly tolerate sorrow in our lives? Perhaps the question ought to be turned upon ourselves: How can we who love greatly ever forget the cost of our happiness upon our parents and family? How can we so rejoice as to forget the aches in the hearts of our dear ones? If we can answer the question put to ourselves, then we begin to have a glimpse into the mystery of God's wonderful love.

Prayer:

Come, Jesus, our Immanuel! Be "God-with-us" in our joys and sorrows. Save us from rejoicing too much and from weeping too much. Be with us in all moments of our life.

December 22

1 Sam 1:24–28. Hannah presents the boy Samuel to the
    Lord at the sanctuary of Shiloh; "he shall be dedicated
    to the Lord as long as he lives."
Luke 1:46–56. While visiting her cousin Elizabeth, Mary
    sings her magnificat, praising God for looking "upon
    his servant in her lowliness."

We find a cycle from death to life in today's scriptural readings about Hannah and about Mary. Each
woman had been without child and in a marvelous way
each was now carrying an infant within her. Elizabeth
despite her advanced age, Hannah despite her seeming
sterility, Mary despite her virginity. God had miraculously intervened and out of death created a new life. The cycle begins all over again. Hannah presents her child
Samuel to the high priest Eli to minister at the sanctuary;
she gives up the child of long desires and fervent prayer.
Mary too would lose her child to a servant-ministry that
would lead to the cross. Yet out of each loss God again
created new life in unsuspecting ways. Through Samuel
God would anoint David as king and institute a royal dynasty. Through Jesus this kingdom would reach out to
embrace the world. Each kingdom, that of David and the
one of Jesus, would experience many moments of death
to new life!

Transitions from death to life, from life to death, are
achieved in the midst of elemental fierceness. At such
crucial moments no one asks any questions or discusses
what is happening. All we can do is to act instinctively
and forcefully according to the most basic laws of human
nature. Second Isaiah once wrote very pointedly if a bit
sarcastically:

Foolish that one who asks a man, "What are you
    begetting?"
    or a woman [in childbirth], "What are you
    giving birth to?"

(Is 45:10)

Jeremiah refers to other iron-clad laws of nature. God is
overheard to say:

I made the sandy shore the sea's limit,
    which by eternal decree it may not overstep.
Toss though it may, it is to no avail;
    though its billows roar, they cannot pass.

(Jer 5:22)

There are eternal decrees governing the border between
sea and land, between life and death, which are nonnego-
tiable. These moments are as "stern as death" (Cant 8:6).
Some of the fierce strokes of this long struggle appear in
Mary's magnificat.

    Mary's hymn probably preexisted in the long hym-
nic tradition of Israel. Its lines were not even composed
originally by Hannah, upon whose canticle the magnificat is carefully modeled. Hannah's song occurs within today's liturgy as the responsorial psalm. Both Hannah's
song and Mary's magnificat say nothing about the birth
of a child marked for greatness but rather exalt an experience common to everyone. Every person at key moments
of life is called by God from death to life, from life to
death. These fierce, demanding moments cannot be
dodged, once they appear before us.

    Although the experience is common in everyone's
life, still the way that Hannah and Mary responded is
highly unique. They prepare us effectively for Christmas,

the birth of Jesus, the transition from death to life. Unusual strength of character appears within each of these women.

Hannah speaks of having "swallowed up my enemies" and Mary of deposing "the mighty from their thrones"; nonetheless, each speaks and acts with exceptional modesty and quiet composure. Hannah says to Eli, the high priest: "Pardon, my Lord! As you live, my Lord, I am the woman who stood near you here, praying . . ." Mary refers to herself as the "servant" whom the Lord "looked upon in her lowliness."

For many reasons a strong humility is required at such traumatic moments as death and birth. First of all, no struggle will stop the process; secondly, the facts are obvious and unchangeable. Greatness depends upon a willing acceptance of the death or the birth, so that a person lives thereafter in full view of eternity. Then too no one can explain what is happening (it is too obvious for explanation) nor can anyone prove its value (as the future is hidden in God's providence). By submitting to this overwhelming plan of God with all the energy at our call, we will discover a strength, an insight, a sense of judgment which will take everyone, including ourselves, totally by surprise.

Hannah sang her song at Shiloh, a spot some forty miles north of Jerusalem, now in such ruins that even an archaeologist has difficulty piecing the bits of rock together. Mary's magnificat was first heard at Ein Karim where the lovely Church of the Visitation stands. Ein Karim is gently tucked away within the steep hills just west of Jerusalem. Death and Life again appear, each in such a quiet way, each overwhelming in its message, each gathered up in the birth of the infant Jesus. At times, Jesus' presence will mean hardship and even desolation, at other times loveliness and peace, but always leading us to eternal exultation and fulfillment of every hope, just as the Lord "promised our ancestors, promised Abraham [and Sarah] and their descendants forever." Mary's prayer will certainly be heard.

Prayer:

Come, King of all nations, for you, Lord Jesus, are a home for each of us in every moment of our existence, sorrowful and joyful. You are the source of your Church's unity and faith. Save all humankind, for we are your own creation. Come, King of all nations.

December 23

Mal 3:1–4, 23–24. Before the great and terrible day of the Lord, God sends into the temple the messenger of the covenant, Elijah the prophet.

Luke 1:57–66. Once John the Baptist is born, Zechariah can speak again. There are outbursts of joy and wonder throughout the countryside.

In the third and last chapter of the prophet Malachi a temple liturgy is reenacted as frightening as any vision can be with divine messengers and awesome people like the prophet Elijah who long ago was taken up into heaven in a whirlwind, with sacrificial fire that can burn away impurities like a fuller's lye. People forget every other distraction like grudges and family feuds, and the hearts of children are turned to their parents and families are reunited.

This final chapter of Malachi once ended, like today's readings, on a note of terrifying destruction:

Lest I come and strike
the land with doom.

These lines also concluded the entire book of the twelve
minor prophets. The rabbis could not bear such gloom at
the end, and so they repeated four lines from an earlier
verse:

Lo, I will send you
Elijah the prophet,
Before the day of the Lord comes,
the great and terrible day.

Other books, like Amos, were also given a happy ending
by a later editor (Am 9:11–15).

For us the joyful conclusion comes in the birth of
John the Baptist. This idyllic scene, unlike the vision of
Malachi, does not take place in the temple, but in the
lovely countryside of Ein Karim. This village lies within
the steep hills immediately west of Jerusalem. On the hillside the exquisite Church of the Visitation marks the traditional place where Elizabeth secluded herself during
her pregnancy and received a visit from Mary. At the
bottom where the hills and roads all converge, the
Church of John the Baptist commemorates the place of
the prophet's birth. Yet, the hills and valleys are so beautiful as to seem to be extensions of the sanctuaries—or
vice versa! One hears the chirping of birds, walks beneath
pomegranate trees, smells the fragrance of ripening
grapes, looks out upon the terraces crisscrossing up the
hillsides. Every step is rich with life. A person hardly
feels the need of temple or church when God's presence
descends from every direction.

All of us know beautiful spots like this. These may be our home or a city park, or they may be friendships which always soothe our troubles, or they may be activities like volunteer work in a hospital. We all have our Ein Karim that draws us away from the hard competition of business and the tense decisions of life, so that we can turn around the bend and descend into our lovely valley of peace.

We all experience another strange phenomenon. Nothing seems to pull us away from God as peace and security. Seldom do we run to a priest or a religious minister and exclaim, "Let us pray because everything is going so beautifully!" Most of us pray more spontaneously in times of trouble: even sin moves us to turn toward God more effectively than virtue!

The book of Malachi then is a necessary warning: do not forget the Creator and Redeemer as you enjoy his lovely earth and relax in his salvation. Sweet joy always contains an element of fear; whatever is more fragile can be lost more easily. We need, therefore, the terrifying vision of Malachi.

We also stand in need of celebrating liturgically what we take for granted in everyday life. It is important that we journey from Ein Karim, up and over the steep hills to Jerusalem till we arrive at the crest, the temple mount. This area marks the end of a long movement upward in the central mountains of the Holy Land. From the temple mountain the terrain tumbles fast and precipitously into the Dead Sea, 1300 feet below sea level. Little wonder also that we feel an overwhelming fear come over us as we take our place before God to worship our Creator and Redeemer.

For the moment, however, Advent brings us back to the family liturgy and to the birth of Jesus.

Prayer:

Lord, I hear you say: "Lift up your heads and see; your redemption is near at hand." Whenever this redemption expresses itself in fragile joy and delicate beauty, keep me fearful lest I forget and easily break what is as lovely as this.

December 24 (Morning Mass)

2 Sam 7:1–5, 8–11, 16. David was not to build a house or temple for the Lord, but the Lord would establish David's house or dynasty in peace forever.

Luke 1:67–79. At the circumcision and naming of John the Baptist, his father Zechariah sang his "Benedictus" in prophetic melody. He blessed God for raising up a Savior and for summoning the child John as his forerunner.

God is about to step into our lives with such brilliant light and overwhelming goodness that everything which we ourselves have already accomplished or which we can promise to do in the future will fade into oblivion. At a time like this we remember Zechariah's hymn:

The Dayspring shall visit us in his mercy
to shine on those who sit in darkness and in the
    shadow of death,
to guide our feet into the way of peace.

Like David in the first reading we realize that God needs none of our actions, least of all our grandiose plans.

After conquering Jerusalem and establishing himself

within the city, David's conscience bothered him. He said to Nathan the prophet, "Here I am living in a house of cedar, while the ark of God dwells in a tent!" Nathan's first response, "Build a temple to the Lord," was reversed the next day. Ever since the Lord brought the Israelites out of Egypt, he has dwelt in a tent. He was not dependent upon King David for a proper dwelling place, but David was totally in need of the Lord. God promised to protect him and his dynasty forever.

Many forces were at work in turning down this request to build a temple. Tradition was one of the strong negative voices. For two or three hundred years, Mosaic religion centered in the ark of the covenant, enshrined within a shepherd's or nomad's tent. This tent could easily be collapsed and rolled up, and carried by the people in their wanderings. God was thus enshrined at the heart of the people's everyday life, moving with every major change in their existence. Still another force worked against the idea of a temple. In the supreme moment of prayer or worship God was not to be dependent upon human prestige or wealth, nor upon status or rank. In that case the temple with its mighty walls and glistening splendor might destroy the sense of faith, the realization of God's sudden and surprising ways of coming to us.

God, therefore, declared that he would build a house or everlasting dynasty for David. Zechariah sang, when he saw in vision the one for whom his own son will prepare the way:

> He has raised up a horn of saving strength for us
>   in the house of David his servant,
> As he promised through the mouths of his holy
>   ones,
> the prophets of ancient times.

In such an unusual way did God fulfill the ancient prophecies. Jesus' claims to the Davidic promises came through his foster-father Joseph; Mary like her cousin Elizabeth descended from a priestly family of the tribe of Levi! The Davidic family had been dethroned centuries ago when Jerusalem was destroyed by the Babylonians (587 B.C.) and had never reappeared, even during the Maccabean wars of independence. Fulfillment would come to the prophet Nathan's words in ways that David never anticipated.

During his entire public ministry Jesus never made any claims to earthly royalty. He deliberately slipped away from a popular attempt to make him king (John 6:15). Jesus spoke of the Kingdom of God, not of the kingdom of David.

When the liturgy links the birth of Jesus with God's refusal that David construct a temple, we are impressed with divine liberty and divine surprises. Just as no sunrise is ever the same as the day before, God never comes the same way again into our lives. As the mixture of clouds and dust, wind currents and temperature is keeping the eastern canopy of the sun in continual movement, likewise there is a ceaseless modulation of details in our lives: people come and go, economy is in flux, physical health and mental peace have their ebb and flow. In this ever changing canvas of lives where the ink never dries but always flows into new colors and directions, God is present.

God can come in every possible human situation. He is not confined to a massive temple. He can pitch his tent and again he can fold it up. He abides with us and he journeys with us. Over and over again he is born, as our own life takes a new fresh start. We will never stop being surprised at God's freedom to be with us. Yet, paradoxically, God's supreme freedom is dependent upon the changing moods of our lives. He must be born according to the laws of our human nature, from the flesh of his mother Mary. Then he will impart "freedom," as Zechariah sang, freedom from sin and servitude.

The sun is about to break through our darkness.

Prayer:

O Christ, radiant Dawn, splendor of eternal light, sun of justice, shine on us, illumine the dark areas of our life and give warmth to our cold hearts. Break our routine of indifference with the splendor of your freedom.

PART TWO

Weekdays of the Christmas Season

December 26—Feast of St. Stephen

Acts 6:8–10; 7:54–59. The martyrdom of St. Stephen.
Matt 10:17–22. Jesus foresees persecution, from one's own nation and even from one's own immediate family, often from people with good motives.

We are startled by the feast of the martyr St. Stephen right after the liturgical celebration of the birth of Jesus. Evidently the tradition of the Church has seen much more in Christmas than the appearance of a new baby, even though this baby be the second person of the Blessed Trinity, one with the Father and the Spirit through all eternity. Mary's child was given the name of Jesus or "Savior" before his birth, so that right from the start Jesus was challenging, threatening and even condemning whatever was sinful or unworthy of God's family.

Stephen took up the task, continuing to judge, argue and debate, publicly and privately, that all the Hebrew Scriptures led to Jesus. His language at times was fierce, hardly adapted to calm and reasonable dialogue. For instance, he completed his discourse before the Sanhedrin by throwing down the gauntlet: "You stiffnecked people, uncircumcised in heart and ears, you are always opposing the Holy Spirit just as your ancestors did before you."

We are still stunned by the violent transition from Christmas to the martyrdom of Stephen. We must live with this question. Even at that other problems arise. Although a temporary persecution and dispersal took place, with a prominent place in this harassment given to Saul of Tarsus, nonetheless we read just two chapters later in the Acts of the Apostles: "Meanwhile throughout all Judea, Galilee, and Samaria the Church was at peace" (Acts 9:31). Our impression is confirmed that Stephen was one of those persons who inevitably stir conflict.

Once he was out of the way, the storm passed and the waters became calm. Just as earlier, we questioned the abrupt change from peaceful Christmas to Stephen's violent martyrdom, now we are baffled by the quick return of peace!

These facts may put other details into proper focus. Those who were stoning Stephen piled their "cloaks at the feet of a young man named Saul." Saul not only approved this execution but he proceeded at once to systematically extend the persecution. Saul shows up later in his letters as a person too good to be acting here out of bad will.

The mystery thickens when we read the Gospel. Jesus speaks of flogging in the synagogues and even of families turning against their own members, parents against their children, children against their parents. Elsewhere, Jesus added that people will think that they are serving God and his cause (John 16:2).

God's ways, especially his providential care of us, slip beyond our comprehension, maybe beyond our acceptance, when we turn the preceding idea around and realize that good will does not prevent a person from making serious mistakes, even mistakes that inflict undeniable hardship upon others. How does God—how do we—deal with a person who thinks to be following the Lord's will and yet is seriously misdirected? The one whom they are persecuting is just and innocent. They are guilty—or it might be more correct to say, responsible—for executing the proto-martyr of Christianity.

What can anyone say in circumstances like these? There is no satisfactory explanation. Therefore, Jesus added:

When the hour comes, you will be given what you are to say. You yourselves will not be the speakers; the Spirit of your Father will be speaking in you.

The shifting scene of any revolution cuts the person loose from set answers. Such would be the situation of Jesus' disciples right after his death. Through the Acts of the Apostles and Paul's epistles to the Galatians and Romans, the early Church was groping, arguing and even summoning a general council (Acts 15) in order to settle serious controversies.

In this sense, we can compare the infant Church to the infant Jesus. Mary and Joseph, the child's mother and foster-father, possessed no pattern and could not turn to an ecumenical council in their charge to raise a child, miraculously conceived, preordained to a messianic mission, the redeemer of its own parents! How Mary and Joseph must have groped for answers, discussed among themselves, prayed most earnestly, and felt humbly crushed by a mission so awesome.

Each of us needs the wisdom to decide when we must speak and when we must simply turn to God's Holy Spirit who will be speaking in us. Nor should we feel abandoned by God if we face situations for which traditions provide no patterns. If we wait prayerfully and trustfully, if we meditate upon the Scriptures and if we seek council from the assembly of believers, eventually the Holy Spirit will lead us forward on the right path. We will also see ourselves in a line of continuity with our ancestors. Then even if people oppose us and persecute us and if they are acting mistakenly under good will, all our questions will not be answered but God's will shall certainly be fulfilled in our lives.

Prayer:
Into your hands, O Lord Jesus, I entrust my spirit.

You hide me in the shelter of your wings from the plottings of evil or badly informed people. Like your first martyr Stephen may I see you at God's right hand at the moment of death and also at all important decisions.

December 27—Feast of St. John, Apostle and Evangelist

1 John 1:1–4. What we have seen, heard and touched we proclaim as the word of life which existed "from the beginning." Through this word you may share life with us and our joy be complete.

John 20:2–8. At Mary Magdalene's announcement that the tomb was empty, Peter and John ran to the tomb. When John entered, he saw and believed.

The opening words of St. John's first epistle seem like an initial attempt of what would later become the formal prologue to the fourth gospel. When John therefore proclaims "what was from the beginning," he was thinking, as he did in the opening lines of his gospel, of the first moments of creation. He is bearing witness to what has existed from all eternity. This word of life consists in what John declared to have seen, heard and touched:—Jesus the word incarnate, but also Jesus as the word announced by ancient prophets and Jesus as the word now preached in the Church. The mystery of Jesus reaches all around us, so that we too can see with our own eyes, look upon and touch with our hands.

That the witness is considerably more than actually living with Jesus during his earthly ministry becomes still more apparent when we move to the Gospel account. What the disciple whom the Lord loved saw in the tomb for the confirmation of his faith was certainly not the body of Jesus. Just the contrary, to have seen the body of Jesus would have disproven the resurrection and made the death of Jesus the final debacle in a glorious but tragic career. John, consequently, was thereafter to be a witness of the risen Jesus whom he did not see, touch or hear!

Why then, did John begin his first epistle by stating that he has seen, touched and heard the word of life that was from the beginning? Without in any way denying that the apostolic witness included their companionship with Jesus during his lifetime, still the apostles insisted much more on Jesus' resurrection and on his sending the Spirit into the midst of the Church. The Holy Spirit would enliven men and women with the attitudes of Jesus, so that others could see in the members of the Church, Christ's body in the language of St. Paul (1 Cor 12), the marvelous revelation of the word of life. The life of each member was to become a revelation of Jesus.

Each new grace in ourselves and in others can be compared to a new birth of Jesus. It may not be improper to continue the image of Jesus' birth as an infant. An infant is to be touched and handled, it is to be carried and fondled, it is to be seen and heard continually for it needs uninterrupted attention. As Jesus is born anew in ourselves or in others, we can tenderly touch, see and hear the word of life. We must listen carefully, for it whispers the deepest desires of God. We must look intently, for there is an ever new revelation of life and growth. There must be continuous attention to this word of life, who is Jesus in our midst.

St. John is frequently given the title, "John the Divine," because of the sublimity of his doctrine. Today's meditation, particularly within the season of Christmas, perceives a wondrous revelation in our very midst, in each one of us. Here is where we receive "what was from the beginning, what we have heard, what we have seen with our eyes, what we have looked upon and our hands have touched—the word of life." Here in the midst of ourselves, the Church, we possess what John realized could not be contained within a tomb. Looking into the tomb and finding it empty, John "saw and believed." He peered into the mystery of Jesus' resurrection and believed in his glorious presence through the Spirit in our midst.

Prayer:

Lord, your apostle John reclined close to you at the Last Supper. To him you communicated heavenly secrets. By our charity and patience may we too recline at your side, be guided by your wisdom and be instruments for others to hear, see and touch the word of life.

December 28—Feast of the Holy Innocents

1 John 1:5—2:2. God is light. If we walk in light and acknowledge our sins, he who is just will cleanse us of every wrong.

Matt 2:13-18. The martyrdom of the Holy Innocents and Rachel's tears for her children.

The Holy Innocents suffered quickly, perhaps unconsciously. It is their parents who felt the most poignant pain from the sword that struck their infants. While the parents felt their own flesh being torn from their bodies in the massacre of the children, these children were seen as helpless victims, frustrated in seeking the normal and beautiful joys of living.

> Rachel mourns her children,
> she refuses to be consoled
> because her children are no more.

Matthew ends right there his quotation from the prophet Jeremiah. The situation does seem hopeless. The allusion to Rachel, in fact, goes back to this favorite wife of the patriarch Jacob who longed for another child. Only after many years did she conceive but then she died in giving birth to Benjamin. "With her last breath . . . she called him Ben-oni [son of my affliction]; his father, however, named him Benjamin [son of my right hand]!" (Gen 35:18). The very name Rachel, therefore, evokes tears.

It is important to continue reading not only in Matthew's gospel but also from the source of his citation in the prophecy of Jeremiah. The prophet immediately adds what is the reason for referring to Rachel's tears:

> Cease your cries of mourning,
> wipe the tears from your eyes.
> The sorrow you have shown shall have its reward,
> they shall return from the enemy's land.
> There is hope for your future, says the Lord;
> your sons shall return to their own borders.
>   (Jer 31:16–17)

Matthew also proceeds on a positive note. He recounts how an angel appeared to Joseph in Egypt with the command: "Get up, take the child and his mother, and set out for the land of Israel."

Here is an excellent example of *midrash,* a popular style of Jewish exegesis. An older biblical text is always quoted, yet not for its own sake but for the application to a later age. Moreover, the principal lines of the citation are omitted and in their place the new meaning or application is provided. Therefore, the main idea in Jeremiah's statement was the return of the exiled people, which Matthew updates in the return or exodus of Jesus out of Egypt. Rachel's tears find their reward!

Midrash is never simple, and in this case we have to understand "exodus" as referring to the death and resurrection of Jesus. Once in exile, Jesus returned to his heavenly home. Now we are at the application to the Holy Innocents. Jesus' exodus meant a resurrection from the dead for all martyrs. From a reading of the longer text of Jeremiah and Matthew, then, we locate the real meaning of the feast of the Holy Innocents in the assurance that *all* suffering will blossom in wonderful new life. Rachel's tears always find their reward through Jesus.

Yet the Scriptures do not deny the reality of sorrow and tragedy. Loyalty to Jesus and to the Church has inflicted extraordinary pain and persecution upon the disciples of the Lord. There is no better word than atrocity for the massacre of little children. Rachel's tears are real. Our tears too are not make-believe. Our tears too may be wrung from us, not so much by our faults and mistakes, as by the injustices and sins of other, bad-intentioned people. Or we may see tragedy, like that forced upon the mothers of the Holy Innocents, due to the pride and jealousy of a ruler like Herod. Our sorrows, moreover, may not bear the noble marks of persecution nor the gracious mark of innocent suffering. We may have caused our sorrows by our personal sins and foolish behavior.

Jesus did not die for the just but for sinners

(Mark 2:17) and he rose from the dead for people guilty of punishment, not worthy of blessing. All sorrow, therefore, can lead not only to joy but also to the innocence of today's saints. We read in today's Scripture:

> If we acknowledge our sins,
> he who is just can be trusted
> to forgive our sins
> and cleanse us from every wrong.

The sorrows, produced by our sins, can be the purifying force, returning us to the innocence of our infancy, yet this time with all the strength and experience of an adult.

Prayer:
   Our soul, Lord, has escaped like a bird from the hunter's net. Keep us worthy of the promised land of peaceful innocence.

December 29—Fifth Day within the Octave of Christmas

1 John 2:3–11. We are to conduct ourselves with love as Jesus did. This commandment is old, but it is also new as realized in Jesus and applied to ourselves.
Luke 2:22–35. In the solemn moment of Jesus' presentation in the temple, Simeon announces him to be "the light to the nations," a sign to be opposed. Because of that antipathy, Mary's heart shall be pierced.

   A sound, practical pedagogy marks John's discourse in his first epistle. Because everyone instinctively reacts against commands and becomes even more stubborn in face of *new* commands, John states simply:

> Dearly beloved, it is no new commandment
> that I write to you, but an old one which you
> had from the start.

John, therefore, is reaching behind the roots and instincts of his readers to what has always existed at the core of their being. "From the start," that is, from the moment of your conception, this law of life directed your most spontaneous and essential activities. We think of an infant—we can make the application to the infant Jesus—who acts without thinking and will quickly become sick or will even die, certainly it will cry with all its tiny might, if these instincts are interfered with.

John was appealing to what the reader—ourselves—can do best and most easily, to what comes by second nature, shall we say by first nature! Already there is a prophetic strain in John's words. The prophets like Amos and Hosea generally did not expend their energy over fine points of the law. They generally avoided any reference to "casuistic laws" (Ex 21–22), a series of examples and norms applying the law to individual cases or new problems. The prophets reached behind these legal solutions to the basic Ten Commandments (Ex 20:1–17) or to the very ancient clan traditions (Deut 25:5–10) which are so simple and so mandatory that they cannot be discussed (Am 2:7–8; Hos 4:1–3). People just do it that way!

John convinces us that we and our ancestors, without batting an eye, have always acted in this way. Admittedly such traditional activity is easy. We and everyone have always done it that way: it is just taken for granted. But John has slipped in another ingredient which is absolutely necessary, in fact, non-negotiable. At this point we

tend to say "No!" John responds that if such is your answer, then you will live in darkness, not knowing where
you are going.

The "new" quality, added by John to the "old" commandment, comes from the presence of Jesus. Jesus has
imparted heroic dimensions and super-human expectations to the "old commandment." No one can claim to be
a follower of Jesus and bypass the extraordinary way by
which Jesus has extended our primary human obligation
of charity, forgiveness and patience far beyond our normal expectation. Jesus presents these norms not as a nice
ideal, nor as a criterion for correct etiquette, but as a
command for everyone of his followers. John wrote:

> The way we can be sure of our knowledge of Je-
> sus is to keep his commandments. The person
> who claims, "I have known him," without
> keeping his commandments, is a liar; in such a
> one there is no truth.

Jesus somehow by his death and resurrection has
made all things new. "To be honest," John seems to admit, "I have to tell you something." He then wrote:

> On second thought, the commandment that I
> write to you is *new,* as it is realized in him and
> in you, . . . for the real light begins to shine.

Jesus, it seems, reveals "new" and hidden parts of our instincts, always with us but never clearly known to exist.
If we are henceforth to walk in the light of Jesus, then we
will have to activate dormant and unused muscles. That
is so difficult, that we think to be destroying ourselves.
We resist. Yet, here is our salvation.

The child Jesus touched people in that way. The old man Simeon humbly confessed that his entire life up to this point could be put aside, so that the most hidden promises of God to the ancestors could blossom:

> Master, you can dismiss your servant in peace;
> you have fulfilled your word.
> For my eyes have witnessed your saving deed. . . .

How heroic is that simple "dismiss in peace!" Most people fear to die. Yet, in this new commandment there lies all the hope for life and goodness.

What Simeon spontaneously and enthusiastically drew into his arms, the child that means his death for the sake of new life, others would reject. He said to Mary, the mother of Jesus, as he glanced at the child in his arms:

> This child is destined to be the downfall and rise of many in Israel, a sign that will be opposed, and you yourself shall be pierced with a sword.

Christmas leaves us with the baffling meditation: how can it be that an innocent child will strike us down and will be the occasion for a sword to pierce our hearts?

To be most alive at the depth of ourselves and so to follow the "new" commandment—yet it was with us from the beginning—we may have to sacrifice everything else. Yet what is deepest at our roots turns out to be our truest self where Jesus creates our new person.

Prayer:

Lord, through your tender compassion, the dawn breaks upon us. In the birth of Jesus, we are reborn to our truest self and in his light we follow the new commandment, a revealing light, a glory, a salvation.

December 30—Sixth Day within the Octave of Christmas*

1 John 2:12–17. The worldly life of pretense is passing away—even if it still has the power to seduce—while the person who follows God's will in this world endures forever.

Luke 2:36–40. Anna, the prophetess, fasting and praying, met the Holy Family as she entered the temple. She talked about the child to all who were looking forward to the deliverance of Jerusalem. Mary and Joseph then returned to Nazareth.

We sense serious tensions in today's readings. John writes of the allurements of the world that can seduce Jesus' followers. John speaks severely about this world; it does more then tempt to sin. Words like "seduce" and "entice" do not imply even a fair contest with sin; people seem to be innocently victimized. Normal people with little religious sophistication could not cope with the wily world. They could not live untainted. They must flee the world or at least live in continual suspicion of it. It would be best if they could find protection in God's eternal word. The home of God's word and of God himself was the temple. Yet, the Holy Family departed from the temple to find their home in Galilee, a place that certainly qualified as part of the secular world!

* When there is no Sunday within the octave of Christmas—that is, when Christmas and New Year's fall on a Sunday—the feast of the Holy Family replaces the prayers and readings of this day.

In the first two chapters of his gospel Luke is implying that the world is not necessarily as "secular" as we imagine! Beautiful liturgies of prayer and divine dialogue take place outside the temple built by human hands but within the temple prepared by God. The temple is the person of Mary whom the Holy Spirit overshadowed as it once dwelt within the tabernacle constructed by Moses (Ex 40:34–38). On the hillsides of Bethlehem angels and shepherds executed liturgy more magnificent than any sacred function in temple or synagogue.

It would seem that the tension is not between living in the world or away from the world, but of transforming the world into a sacred place through the presence of Jesus. Yet if Jesus changes our secular world into a temple, we are not at all being asked to stop all secular occupations and to perform only sacred rituals. In other words, our home and place of work remain a home and a place of work, a playground is still a recreational area. None of these spots is to be remodeled into a shrine or church! It is the presence of Jesus that makes the difference.

We will not be enticed innocently into sin, nor must we remain always suspicious that someone is trying to trap us into evil. Rather than be at a severe disadvantage by our innocence and simplicity, these attitudes unite us immediately with Jesus. Our directness enables us clearly to say "Yes" or "No" (Matt 5:37), quickly to go the extra mile (Matt 5:41), to be the happiest in giving away our coat as well as our shirt (Matt 5:40). Blessed are we at such moments; the Lord is reigning in our midst.

Just as the presence of Jesus does not demand that we change our normal "worldly" setting into a shrine or temple, neither does Jesus intend to do away with temples, synagogues and churches! The temple occupies a very important place in Luke's infancy narrative. The climax takes place with Jesus' presentation in the temple (Luke 2:22–40). It was in the synagogue of Nazareth that Jesus solemnly began his public ministry and gave his inaugural address (Luke 4:16–22) and finally at the end of Luke's gospel the disciples "were to be found in the temple constantly speaking the praises of God" (Luke 24:53).

Without temple, shrine or church we become worldly and materialistic, earthbound and time-limited. Because time is running out on us and the amount of space on planet earth is dwindling, we become suspicious of others. We build up our defenses and seek ways to trap others—before they ensnare us. We become the force by which the world seduces and entices others. We begin to seduce ourselves!

Turning the tables around, we find how much the sacred liturgy of the temple or church depends upon the world which surrounds it. Unless the church celebrates something real, unless liturgy brings before God the important moments of births, weddings, ordinations, religious consecrations and deaths, unless we feel at home in church commemorating great anniversaries and praying for serious needs, then church is a facade, liturgy is empty and the entire ceremony is a whitewash.

Like Anna then we need to come constantly to the temple and it is important that the Scriptures inspire us to fast and pray. Like the Holy Family we will proceed from temple to our place in the world, to our Nazareth. We will not be fearful of a "seductive" world but will peacefully grow in wisdom, strength and grace.

Prayer:

Lord, we bring the gifts of our labor and play into your holy temple. We bring the gifts of your Scripture and inspiration from your temple into our daily lives.

Thus our world is made firm and you govern our lives with justice and goodness.

December 31—Seventh Day within the Octave of Christmas

1 John 2:18–21. In this "final hour," antichrists have risen out of the midst of Jesus' own disciples. His true followers have the anointing of the Holy One.

John 1:1–18. In the prologue to his gospel John contrasts light and darkness! The Word, shining in the world is not overcome by darkness but becomes incarnate in our midst and shares his fullness with us.

On this last day of the calendar year (the Church year begins with the first Sunday of Advent) our readings from the First Epistle of John confront us with the "final hour" of the antichrists. This serious challenge is well chosen as the secular world rings out the old year this night. Very truly we are at the "final hour."

The author of this epistle spoke from his own time when many Christians expected the end of the world and the second coming of Christ at any moment. "Antichrists" could arise because people were waiting for Christ. For any number of unworthy reasons whether these be personal gain, bad theology or religious drive, certain persons would make the most of the situation by claiming to be the Christ or at least his representative. A cult would form around them. This expectation of Christ had crested in its enthusiasm several times over. Paul was responsible for stirring it up in his First Letter to the Thessalonians; he then had to calm and control the fanaticism by writing a Second Letter to the Thessalonians and by further statements in his correspondence with the Corinthians (2 Thess 2; 1 Cor 7).

No one can deny that crises occur and these can seem like the end of the world. These crucial turning points can direct us toward a marvelous opportunity or toward a catastrophe. In the first case we speak of a "conversion" or a "born again" experience. We can be so overwhelmed that we will grope for the right words and may even say that Christ appeared to us or that it was the Lord who intervened.

These episodes may be confined to an individual person, family or religious community. Sometimes when a large area or nation is gripped in crises, everyone is expected to think and act heroically and to be ready for the manifestation of the Lord. These are times when no one can respond with small talk and routine actions. Every moment takes on the proportions of a battle with Goliath. Within early Christianity the whole Church was plunged into persecution and traumatic decisions. One of these moments was the break with the Jewish ancestral religion to which Jesus belonged, another of course was the Roman persecution. Still other catastrophes exploded in the midst of the first disciples of Jesus like the Roman destruction of Jerusalem in 70 A.D. The early Church, therefore, was frequently swept with apocalyptic movements and with keen expectations of the second coming, as though "the final hour" were really at hand.

John's gospel, on the other hand, has put these movements and ideas aside and has settled down with the Church, its sacraments and the symbolic remembrances of Christ's presence. Rather than wait expectantly for the second coming, the Church worships the Lord mystically present in the sacraments and in the word. As we read in today's gospel:

The Word became flesh
and made his dwelling among us,
and we have seen his glory.

The word is in our midst, gloriously celebrated.

This mystical presence of the Lord, now in the sacraments and in the preaching of the Church, challenges us. Each of us and at times all of us together face serious problems and we seem engulfed by darkness. John writes again:

Whatever came to be in him, found life,
life for the light of men.
The light shines on in darkness,
a darkness that did not overcome it.

All of us will eventually face serious sickness and death. How we react to earlier crises in our life will determine how well we will meet the second coming of the Lord in our passing from this life to eternity.

Perhaps we can look upon the end of the year and the ringing in of the new year as a small crisis. We must face up to our responsibilities and failures over the past three hundred and sixty-five days. The Lord comes again in the new year. Has our (my) handling of the questions, problems and emergencies of the past year enabled us (me) to realize more fully and more deeply the presence of the Lord in my (our) life? Do I place more faith in his power to overcome darkness? Can I confess to have seen more of his glory? Have I shared his love?

Prayer:

Lord Jesus, born in our midst as one of us, you drew us together as your brothers and sisters, all of us children of God. May we learn to welcome you into our midst as a member of our family. May we see ourselves as members of your family. Then your wonderful counsel will direct us in the surprising and even convulsive turning point of our life.

January 2*

1 John 2:22–28. Let the anointing of what you have received remain in your heart. You have no need for anyone to teach you further. Remain in Christ, so that when he appears, you may be fully confident.

John 1:19–28. John the Baptist denied that he was the Mesiah or Elijah or the prophet. He was a voice crying out in the desert, preparing the way of the Lord.

Each reading anticipates the coming of the Lord. In the first reading, we are advised:

Remain in him now, little ones,
so that *when he reveals himself,*
we may be fully confident.

John the Baptist identified his own mission as

A voice in the desert, crying out:
make straight the way of the Lord.

It seems that Jesus must come again and again, Christmas by Christmas, new year by new year. It is always the

*The meditations marked January 2 to January 7 are for weekdays before the celebration of the feast of Epiphany.

same Lord Jesus but it is always a different set of circumstances to which Jesus adapts himself. This diversity also shows up in the two readings for today.

John the Baptist made ready the way of the Lord by simplicity, directness and humility, by austerity and a call to conversion. He made no pretense of being anyone special, certainly not the Messiah, nor Elijah nor one of the prophets. We know, however, that he was the greatest of all the prophets and the immediate precursor of the Messiah. He had no name or title for himself. He was simply a person who did what he felt compelled to do by the Lord. He reached into the book of Isaiah for a passage to describe himself; he had no words of his own. Even this passage was frequently cited at Qumran among the Dead Sea Scrolls. What prepared these Jewish covenanters was the Torah of Moses and its continual study! What they expected was its perfect fulfillment. John the Baptist turned attention from the law to the Giver of the law.

John signals for conversion in a direct way. He had quick, decisive answers for the crowds, the tax collectors and the soldiers. He was convinced of the urgency with which everyone must act. The one to come after him already has

> his winnowing-fan ... in his hand to clear the threshing floor and gather the wheat into his granary; but the chaff he will burn in unquenchable fire (Luke 3:17).

John had little patience for involved theological questions. He never bothered asking himself whether tax collectors were ceremonially clean or not, nor did he first query the soldiers about their position on peace and war!

He said directly to them: "Don't bully anyone. Denounce no one falsely. Be content with your pay." On the contrary, the Qumran covenanters were extremely careful about ceremonial cleanliness and other sectarian questions.

The First Letter of John is preoccupied with theological questions and moves our discussion away from John the Baptist and in the direction of Qumran. This Letter faces up to some of the early heresies within the Church. The relation of Jesus to God the Father and God the Holy Spirit had to evolve theologically beyond the Old Testament and even beyond the teaching of Jesus. The Church was obligated to position herself ever more clearly and forcefully. She would not tolerate any secret way to salvation, called *gnosis,* available only to a select group. Everyone has received the Spirit and therefore has no need of these gnostic secrets.

Sometimes there is need for long patience as we work our way through a complicated problem. God may expect each of us in a group to be honest in dialogue, tolerant in listening, united with the Church at large in our final conclusions. At other times we do not have the luxury of long discussion, but like John the Baptist we cut through the verbiage and demand action at once. Each prepares the way of the Lord, each is adapted to different situations.

It may be that the First Letter of John is better adapted to the beginning of a new year. We feel that we have much time and the long winter to think and discuss. In fact, an entire year lies ahead of us to work through our problems. Yet, we must be ready always for a John the Baptist to appear suddenly, crying out in what has become the desert wilderness of our existence: at once prepare the way of the Lord.

Prayer:

Lord you make known your salvation in the sight of the nations. It is no secret power reserved to your initiated friends. My heart breaks into song and I welcome you at each moment of my life.

January 3

1 John 2:29—3:6. See what love .. we are children of God and we shall see him as he is. Everyone who has this hope based on God keeps himself pure and does not sin.

John 1:29–34. John prepares for the one to come after him, upon whom the Spirit rests. John testifies that such a person is God's chosen one.

John the Baptist's entire ministry was dedicated to preparing for someone else! John quickly pointed out Jesus as the lamb of God upon whom the Spirit rested. John bowed out and even let Jesus gather some of his first disciples from those people who clustered around himself. It was not that John was a failure and had to make a deal with Jesus. Nor was John confused, for his language remained clear and direct.

Humanly speaking then it was not easy for John to admit:

After me is to come a person
who ranks ahead of me,
because he was before me.

With such simplicity and straight talk, John the Baptist urged the crowds to follow Jesus. The question comes to our mind: do we have the same generous spirit to allow someone else to pick up our best ideas and run with them? Are we as openhearted as John and therefore just as contented that others will benefit and even get the credit? John, it is important to remember, was not tossing leftovers but giving up the best to Jesus. Jesus, moreover, would develop John's ideas in new ways. Do we have the patience and cheerfulness to see our best and most creative plans turned around by others to fit the group project?

What we are facing here is the transition from one generation to another or from one member of a family to another. This change is always difficult and it is often the beginning of the end of a good friendship. Or the older person watches over the shoulder of the younger and acts as though still in charge!

The generous spirit of John the Baptist will purify our hearts. We think of a line in the first reading:

> Everyone who has this hope based on him [Jesus] keeps himself pure, as he is pure.

To share this openly with others is bound to rid our hearts of selfishness and ruthless ambition. And in a true sense we do not lose anything or anyone. Rather our ideas are enriched and balanced by the contributions of others, our love brings back to us a contentment and peace beyond explanation.

This mysterious delight and this broadened wisdom have many of the qualities of seeing God face to face. The first reading assures us that "we shall see him as he is." Charity, therefore, imparts a perception of God beyond words, in fact it gives a sense of God's presence that is the closest thing on earth to seeing God "as he is."

Such charity as we are discussing here also enables us to see a vision of Jesus in our neighbors. We acquire a "good eye" always to see the wholesomeness, the honesty and the uprightness of others. By our overlooking their faults, they will tend more and more to live up to our good expectations for them. To be united in such charity is to be united in God and to taste immediately the kindliness of the Lord.

What John the Baptist accomplished so heroically in giving up all for Jesus, the Lord Jesus also manifested in his own self-giving. After his death he put supreme decision-making in the control of the apostles and elders. He accepted what they decided. But a better image may be that of a child. Jesus, the infant born at Christmas, had to comply with the decisions and directions of his parents for many years to come. Yet they too would have to bow to Jesus even before he began his public ministry: "Did you not know I had to be in my Father's house?" (Luke 2:49) and during his apostolate he again seemed to place the needs of the people anxious for his word before the wishes of his mother and brothers and sisters. This response of Jesus, sent through a disciple to his mother Mary, must have hurt her (Mark 3:31–35).

John's advice, like the process of purification at any time, is difficult, in fact heroic. Yet only in this way is our heart renewed and our eyes made ready to see God.

Prayer:

Lord God, keep me always conscious that I form one family with your beloved son Jesus and that I share this privilege with all your other children. Then I will be able quickly to share everything with my family and be enriched by what I give away. I will see you ever more clearly, face to face, through the purity of my love.

January 4

1 John 3:7–10. No one begotten of God can act sinfully;
    the one who acts in holiness is holy as the Son is holy.
John 1:35–42. Two disciples of John the Baptist seek out
    Jesus. One of them, Andrew, brings his brother Simon
    whom Jesus proceeded to name Cephas, an Aramaic
    word meaning "rock." Peter is the Greek or Latin
    form for "rock."

John's gospel fills a lacuna in the synoptic gospels of
Matthew, Mark and Luke. Although these other gospels
begin Jesus' public ministry with his call of the first disciples up north in Galilee, John anticipates that moment
down south near the spot where the Jordan empties into
the Dead Sea. Here the Qumran covenanters lived in
caves and assembled in a complex network of buildings
for ritual baths, eating and work. Here too John the Baptist may have lived for a while with the Qumran group;
some of John's disciples like Andrew and John may have
followed the Baptist when he drifted away from Qumran
to preach and baptize. The episode in today's Gospel enables us to appreciate the noticeable influence of Qumran
upon the preaching of Jesus and eventually upon the
fourth gospel. The apostle Paul also writes with ideas and
phrases which echo in the Dead Sea Scrolls.

While the encounter of Andrew, John and Cephas
with Jesus looks decisively to the future—already Simon
is given a new name and thereby an important role or
new vocation in the plans of Jesus—still we cannot help
but be impressed with the long, careful preparation. God
was drawing together many lines of religious development, like the Jerusalem priesthood in the person of
Zechariah, father of the Baptist, or the Qumran cov-

enanters in serious disagreement with the Sadducee-priests of Jerusalem, or the revival of biblical prophecy in John the Baptist, or the strong messianic hopes expressed in the Qumran group, the zealots and other less known movements. Each of these lines reached back into the ancestral religion, each was immersed in the ancient Scriptures. In fact, at Qumran a quorum of ten men rotated through three shifts of eight hours each, reciting the Torah continually—in fulfillment of God's word in Joshua 1:8,

> Keep this book of the law on your lips.
> Recite it by day and by night.

Qumran looked toward the perfect obedience of the law and its glorious fulfillment.

Already in the first reading for these days of the new year there has been an allusion to "the beginning":

> Let what you have heard from the beginning
> remain in your hearts. (Jan 2)
> The devil is a sinner from the beginning. (Jan 4)

"Beginning," particularly in the writings of St. John generally reaches back before the origin of the universe to the timelessness of eternity where the "Word" dwelt with God the Father (John 1:1). Elsewhere in the Bible "beginning" refers to prophecies already fulfilled and therefore to a security in God as our promised Savior (Is 41:4, 26; 48:3, 12–13). We are impressed how carefully God was preparing for the ultimate fulfillment of prophecy, of religious institutions and of his own eternal plans.

John's gospel has caught the contemplative mood of this long arrangement and direction of history when he records the conversation:

> Andrew and John said to Jesus: "Rabbi,
>   where do you stay?"
> Jesus answered with an invitation:
>   "Come and see."

With a delicate touch of mystery the Gospel concludes the conversation:

> So they went to see where he was lodged and
> stayed with him that day. (It was about four in
> the afternoon.)

Never could they forget the hour of the day that changed their entire life.

This moment with Jesus revamped the entire course of the Bible and yet fitted in very well with the earthly ways of its history. Salvation, in the centuries of Old Testament readiness and in its fulfillment, did not consist in any secret knowledge or *gnosis* nor in privileged rank but in the necessity to "act in holiness." Neither did salvation summon to ceaseless activity. All of human thoughts and deeds were to flow from an inner source of life "because each of us remains of God's stock." The Greek phrase reads literally "God's seed" or "God's nature."

Despite this rootedness in God, we are also surrounded by darkness and the temptations of the devil. This fact too has reached throughout the Scriptures back to the "beginning." The fulfillment of prophecy had to contend with colossal manifestations of evil. This clash of light and darkness is frequently met in John's gospel and in the writings of Qumran.

Therefore, in one sense we ought to act spontaneously in a godly way, yet we are always faced with tempta-

tion and with the fact of evil. The first reading ends with
the way that Jesus summed up his own teaching: to love
one's brother and sister (1 John 3:10).

Prayer:

Lord, enable us to appreciate the power of goodness
within us, rooted as it is in your divine nature, in ancient
Scriptures and in the Father's eternal hopes. Help us to
act in holiness just as you are holy.

January 5

1 John 3:11–21. Loving our brother and sister is our way
of knowing that we are committed to the truth and are
at peace with God, "no matter what our conscience
may charge us with."

John 1:43–51. Jesus called Philip and Nathanael and
promised the latter that he would see angels ascend
and descend upon the Son of Man.

Love and hate, as all the world knows, motivate us
for the most heroic and the most devastating actions.
Hating his brother, Cain proceeded to ensnare and mur-
der him. In the time of Jesus many stories evolved
around Cain and Abel and these find an echo not only in
today's first reading but also in the first eucharistic
prayer:

Look with favor on these offerings and accept
them as once you accepted the gifts of your servant Abel.

Loving others, on the contrary, enables us to "pass

from death to life." It accomplishes the impossible, to bring the dead back to life; it also achieves what may be still more impossible, to love and pray for our enemy (Matt 5:43). In this way we have come to know the love of Jesus for us.

This love abides with us—yesterday's reading called it the "seed of God"—and from these deep interior roots extraordinary acts of helpfulness and concern spring forth. As the first reading states:

> Little children,
> let us love in deed and in truth
> and not merely talk about it.
> This is our way of knowing we are committed
>   to the truth
> and are at peace before him.

Others will take us by surprise in their heroic gestures of kindness. We could never have anticipated it. There will be an interchange between heaven and earth in this manifestation of God's fervor in human words and deeds. Jesus put it this way in speaking with Nathanael:

> I solemnly assure you, you shall see the sky
> opened and the angels of God ascending and
> descending on the Son of Man.

This image comes from the Old Testament account of the patriarch Jacob (Gen 28:10–17). He was beginning his journey to the distant north, fearful for his life because of the jealous hatred of his twin brother Esau (again the Cain and Abel antagonism) and because of the hazards of strange country and foreign people. Through this vision God assured Jacob of divine protection and of blessings beyond his hopes and imagination. When Jacob returned from the north twenty years later, he was already the father of eleven sons. The twelfth, Benjamin, would be born soon after his return to Canaan (Gen 29–30;31:38).

We too possess the nature or seed of God within us, individually and collectively. God has made us one family. To recognize and love every man and woman as brother and sister releases extraordinary energy and exceptional insights within us. It summons us to new actions and "vocations." Like Nathanael we will see angels ascending and descending. Like Jacob we will be strengthened for very difficult actions and blessed beyond our merit. Secret perceptions of goodness in others and in ourselves will be intuited, and Jesus will be whispering, "I saw you under the fig tree"—i.e., I was with you as you dreamed these good deeds and nourished these lovely hopes for others!

Jesus also said of Nathanael, "This man is a real Israelite. There is no guile in him." We too will find ourselves surrounded with innocence and spontaneous goodness. We will feel ourselves immediately in God's presence, face to face, as Jacob confessed:

> Truly, the Lord is in this spot. . . . How awesome is this shrine! This is nothing else but an abode of God, that is, the gateway to heaven (Gen 28:17).

Sometimes, in popular tradition, the word "Israelite" was understood to mean the vision of God.

Charity such as this and its concomitant vision of God will convince us beyond all doubt that our hearts are at peace with God. "Truly the Lord is in this place"—in my heart and in the environment of my life. In this way we can interpret those other words in today's first reading:

> We are at peace before him
> no matter what our consciences may charge us
>   with;
> for God is greater than our hearts
> and all is known to him.

Prayer:

Lord Jesus, you have been born anew, liturgically in the commemoration of your birth at Christmas, realistically in each movement of grace. Keep our hearts without guile, our actions ever obedient to your inspiration, our ideals reaching like the angels from earth toward heaven.

January 6

1 John 5:5–13. We who believe that Jesus is the Son of
    God, have conquered the world. There are three that
    testify to this: the Spirit, water and blood.
Mark 1:7–11. When Jesus was baptized by John, the sky
    was rent, the Spirit descended upon him, and a voice
    from the heavens declared, "You are my beloved Son."

So many biblical passages and traditions converge within today's readings one would think that we are at the end rather than at the beginning of Jesus' public ministry.

Liturgically in the Church Year we are approaching the feast of Epiphany which combines three major mysteries: the manifestation of Jesus as messiah to the three magi who represent the Church's mission to the gentile world; the baptism of Jesus which signals the beginning of his public ministry; and the marriage feast of Cana which symbolizes the mystical union of Jesus with the Church, particularly in the Eucharist. Just as water was made into wine at Cana, in the Eucharist wine is transformed into the blood of Jesus. The first reading is very conscious of the richness of the faith and of its many, overwhelming expressions in the life of every faithful Christian.

We are at the end of a long preparation and at the beginning of a new life that springs from the roots of the old but far surpasses it. The greatest of the Old Testament prophets declared to his own disciples when Jesus approached him:

> I am not fit to stoop and untie his sandal straps.
> I have baptized you in water; he will baptize
> you in the Holy Spirit.

The growth of Jesus' ministry and of the Church's apostolate out of the earlier Scriptures is seen in still other ways, particularly in today's gospel account. Mark relates that "the sky [was] rent in two." The central word "rent" is drawn from the ancient Greek translation of Is 63:19. Within Is 63:7—64:11, the people had been praying intensely, almost in desperation:

> Look down from heaven and regard us . . .
> Where is your . . . surge of pity and your mercy?
> Were Abraham not to know us, . . .
> You, Lord, are our father. . . .
> Why do you let us wander, O Lord, from your
> ways?

> (Is 63:15–17)

Then they shout at the distant, cloudless expanse of the near eastern skies,

> Oh, that you would *rend* those heavens and come down, with the mountains quaking before you (Is 63:19).

This prayer ends with tragic passion, hoping against the impossible:

> Can you hold back, O Lord, after all this? Can you remain silent, and still afflict us so severely? (Is 64:11).

The final question manifesting human desperation close to despair, was incorporated into the Bible and so became God's word to us in our desperation today. This word was spoken to us when it became incarnate in our midst with the presence of Jesus at the Jordan River, asking John to baptize him. John could not hold back, the Heavenly Father could not remain silent any longer, the heavens would be rent. The distant loneliness of earth would become the home of the Spirit as it comes down to rest upon Jesus. The sins of generations are washed away through the baptism of Jesus, and the earlier words within the people's passionate prayer were reversed:

> They rebelled and grieved his Holy Spirit (Is 63:10).

Still other biblical traditions resonate in Mark's account of Jesus' baptism. "Dove" may symbolize not just the Spirit but also the life of the Spirit within the community of Israel. In both Psalm 68:14 and Hosea 11:11 the assembly of God's redeemed people is described as "doves." Mark already sees the new Israel of the Church gathering around Jesus; by baptism they enter the congregation of God's chosen people. Finally, the statement of the Heavenly Father combines the formula of Psalm 2 for enthroning a new king with that of Isaiah for summoning the Suffering Servant to silent humiliation and total rejection:

> You are my chosen son (Ps 2:7). On you my favor rests (Is 42:1–4; 52:13; 53:12).

This rich and mysterious theology requires a lifetime of meditation. At our early baptism little did we know what was happening, no more than a child is conscious as it comes forth from its mother's womb and begins to live. Yet, through the Church's liturgy, we have the opportunity to contemplate year after year the marvelous testimony of the Spirit, the water and the blood. The *Spirit* fulfills the memory of the Scriptures and answers our most desperate prayers. The *Water* of Baptism introduces us into the eternal life shared with Jesus, God's incarnate Word. *Blood* symbolizes the fullness of life and the consummate love of Jesus crucified. There on the cross after his death, "one of the soldiers thrust a lance into his side, and immediately blood and water flowed out" (John 19:34).

We believe in the wondrous life of Father, Son and Spirit within us. Statements of faith, like the Scriptures in today's liturgy, are intended to keep us in living communication with the three persons of the one God. Today's first reading concludes:

> I have written this to you to make you realize

that you possess eternal life . . . in the name of
the Son of God.

Prayer:

O God, rend the heavens again and come down
upon us. Through the anointing of your Holy Spirit and
our loving union with Jesus, we will welcome the thrust
of the soldier's lance, so that we too can testify by blood
(the loving gift of our life) and water (the faith of our
baptism).

January 7

1 John 5:14–21. "God hears us whenever we ask for any-
    thing according to his will." Because we are begotten
    of God, we should pray for our neighbor and not com-
    mit sin. We live in Jesus, who is our true God and eter-
    nal life.
John 2:1–12. The marriage feast at Cana.

Today the Church completes her preparation for the
feast of the Epiphany which celebrates three mysteries in
the life of Jesus, very closely linked with the apostolate of
the Church: the manifestation of Jesus as Messiah to the
Magi and through them to the gentile world; the baptism
of Jesus as a forerunner of our baptismal entry into the
Church; and the marriage feast of Cana as the symbol of
Jesus' spousal union with the Church, of his eucharistic
union with us and of his consummate love on the cross.

The first reading concludes the First Letter of John
which we have been following since December 27th.
Throughout this letter we sense the preoccupation of the
Church with true doctrine and the Church's equal con-

cern to center our faith in the person of Jesus rather than in doctrinal statements. This First Letter has argued against gnostic heretics who claimed that we are not saved by the public preaching of the Church but by secret truths imparted only to the initiated, inner group. Other false teachers attempted to belittle Jesus by identifying themselves or someone else as the true christ; John castigated them as antichrists. Others were upsetting the Church with such emphasis upon the imminent second coming of Jesus that good moral living and the normal care for one's neighbor seemed totally superfluous. Three times, therefore, in this conclusion to the First Letter, we read the phrase, "we know" and therefore let us not wander away in some strange, secret or exotic way!

The marriage feast of Cana enabled the gospel of John to develop a rich theological symbol of the Church and specifically of the Church's principal sacrament, the Eucharist. First of all, we note the close connections with John's account of the death of Jesus. Jesus first declined to do anything at Cana because "my hour has not yet come." The "hour" of Jesus was his glorification through the cross and resurrection (John 12:23–36). Yet at Cana by turning water into wine he anticipated the cross where water and blood flowed from his side and the Eucharist where we partake of the body broken yet glorified and of the blood shed yet the source of life.

Mary was prominently present at Cana when Jesus was glorified by the first sign, again she was beside the cross of Jesus when he was lifted up to draw everyone to himself (John 12:32; 19:25), and finally she was with the disciples in the upper room at the coming of the Holy Spirit (Acts 1:14). Her intercessory prayer is thus carefully linked with the Church.

This biblical and liturgical concern for the Church

enables us to examine our loyalty of faith and discipline. Most of all, I must ask if I identify church with the person of Jesus? Church is not a series of doctrines to be believed or a code of morals to be followed; neither is Church confined to its ordained leaders. Church is the body of Christ; Church is the assembly of the faithful whose life and attitudes, hopes and final glory have been radically transformed by Jesus' personal presence. Church is the wellspring of charity, overflowing with the abundance of the water changed into wine far beyond the needs of the guests, flowing with blood and water from the open side and pierced heart of believers, gathering people as one family round the eucharistic table, awaiting the coming of the Holy Spirit and the ascension into glory with Jesus.

Church is the family, seemingly gathered in the random way that everyone in a village comes to a wedding banquet yet each one solicitous about the others. Church is the family that centers in Jesus through the intercessory prayer of Mary. Jesus certainly is the savior who changes water into wine, is lifted up on the cross, is taken gloriously to heaven and sends the Holy Spirit upon his disciples. Yet we cannot miss the role of Mary, interceding for the miracle which inaugurates Jesus' public ministry, standing at the foot of the cross to receive the final instructions of Jesus, uniting the disciples in the upper room, some in fear but all in expectation of the Holy Spirit. Do I identify church not only with Jesus as Savior but also with Mary as the unifying and solicitous mother?

Prayer:

Lord, you created the family as the home of love, loyalty and concern unto death. Grant that our families ever be an inspiration and model of what is church and that the Church continually offer to our families the nourishing strength of Eucharist and prayer. May Mary continue to intercede for us the Church as she did at the marriage feast of Cana, next to the cross of Jesus on Calvary and in the upper room.

Monday after Epiphany

1 John 3:22—4:6. The early Church, according to this passage, was struggling over false teachers and antichrists who denied the reality of Jesus' incarnation. God's true disciples hear his voice and God answers their prayers.

Matt 4:12–17, 23–25. A great light shines over Galilee as Jesus announces the good news, heals the sick and attracts a large following. Matthew is preparing for Jesus' great Sermon on the Mount.

Both readings combine a strong interior faith with a practical manifestation of that faith. We also glimpse extraordinary miracles within the normal routine of daily living. These reflections flow spontaneously from the mystery of Jesus' birth at Christmas and his glorious manifestation at Epiphany. They also prepare us for the "ordinary" cycle of the Church Year which will begin in about a week. Once Advent and the Christmas-Epiphany season are completed, the Church settles down to a series of thirty-four weeks. At the end of this series, another Church Year will begin with the first Sunday of Advent.

During this week after Epiphany we are being prepared for what is most basic in the life of every disciple of Jesus yet also the cause of serious tension. We are expected to live normal human lives and yet seek ideals which exceed the powers of our mind and sweep even beyond our dreams. We are asked to achieve humanly what lies beyond our human ability.

As a result of the tension two major types of heresies can appear within the history of the Church. One of these heresies so emphasizes the divinity of Jesus that salvation is achieved only by a secret gnostic doctrine and a gift of the Spirit separate from that bestowed upon all Christians at baptism. The other false doctrine so affirms the humanity of Jesus as to deny his preexistence before the incarnation and his equality with the Father and the Holy Spirit. It is far easier either to deny the dignity of the flesh by some kind of false supernaturalism or to canonize it as all-sufficient by a false humanism than to harmonize the human with the divine in our existence. Christianity seriously affirms the divine value of our human nature yet also declares that our humanity will collapse unless God wondrously intervenes. We must seek humanly what only God can enable us to achieve!

Heresies then strike at the central mystery of Christianity, the incarnation of the divine eternal Word, Jesus physically born of Mary. In today's first reading, the clear statement of faith is made:

> Every spirit that acknowledges Jesus Christ
> come in the flesh belongs to God,
> *while every spirit that fails to acknowledge*
> *him* does not belong to God.
> Such is the spirit of the antichrist.

In fact, some early Church fathers read the middle or italicized line of this statement even more forcefully:

> *while every spirit that dissolves him*
> does not belong to God.

During the coming thirty-four weeks of the Church Year we are asked to affirm and strengthen the mystery of Jesus' incarnation by consecrating to God every faculty or member of the human body. We will walk our earthly way yet look with eyes of divine kindliness. With our human hands we will touch others with godly tenderness. Like Jesus in fulfillment of the prophecy of Isaiah, we ought to be God's instrument by which a great light shines upon a people otherwise living in darkness. Then the message of Jesus can be repeated:

Reform your lives—by the good use of
   human talents and potential.
The Kingdom of heaven is at hand—right in the
   midst of your daily human existence.

As Jesus preached in this way the good news of the kingdom, he also cured the people of every disease and illness. Here we see the manifestation of his divinity and the expectation of super-human ideals in our earthly lives. We imitate Jesus by believing in miracles and by the conviction that every human disability will be removed and every tear will be wiped from the eyes (Rev 7:17). If darkness descends, as it did upon the land of Zebulun and Naphtali, heathen Galilee in Isaiah's prophecy, then we believe that through Jesus a new light will shine. Every sorrow is to prepare for a greater manifestation of Jesus. We ought to communicate such extraordinary hope that we will attract people to Jesus, no matter what the cost in human endurance.

Prayer:
   Lord Jesus, enable us to profess our faith in your incarnation by the dignity and respect we show to our hu-

man bodies. Increase our faith in your divinity so that the manifestation of your divine glory will enhance our hopes and lead to our bodily resurrection with you. We thank you, Lord, for the mysteries of your incarnation and epiphany.

Tuesday after Epiphany

1 John 4:7–10. God is love and has first loved us. Therefore we ought to love one another according to a love revealed in Jesus, God's own son sent into our midst.

Mark 6:34–44. Jesus multiplied bread and fish for more than five thousand people; they had seemed like sheep without a shepherd.

Love and hatred rank among the most normal human reactions. Each of these responses comes so spontaneously that it happens before we think about it. There seems to be a more direct line of communication between our environment and our heart than with our mind or any other human faculty. We can step into a room and know at once whether we like or dislike the people! Later we think about the reasons and seek to justify the reaction of our heart.

Jesus too reacted intuitively. His human emotions, moreover, had been elevated and transformed by his divinity. As his arms reached out with human tenderness to touch a sick person, divine power surged through them to cure the illness. In today's gospel the opening line proclaims how divine were the human emotions of Jesus. "Jesus saw a vast crowd. *He pitied them.*" Without preparing the disciples for what was to follow, he says simply: "Give them something to eat." While Jesus was acting on the emotional level of compassion, they were reacting on the rational level of practicality. They responded: "Are we to go and spend two hundred days' wages for bread to feed them?" They told Jesus that there was a limit to what could be spent for the poor and the needy, and two hundred days' wages was too much! We see, therefore, that Jesus almost got caught by his emotions before he knew clearly what he would do. The following miracle is thus seen as a tribute to his compassion rather than as a manifestation of his power.

Jesus' style of acting is presented as a model for our faith and imitation. Otherwise it would never have been recorded in the gospel. In still another way the gospel text insists that we too, like Jesus, must follow the lead of our love and compassion. All of these reactions are absorbed within the Church's liturgy.

The gospel account represents a mingling of traditions about Jesus' life with the eucharistic liturgy of the early Church. Like a liturgical service the people in the gospel account take their places in an orderly way of hundreds and fifties. The "church" does not resemble the disorderly way that five thousand people would scatter over the hillside for a picnic. Mark even speaks of their being "neatly arranged like flower beds." The liturgical tone becomes still clearer in the eucharistic phrases: "Jesus . . . raised his eyes to heaven, pronounced a blessing, broke the loaves, and gave them to the disciples to distribute."

The eucharistic setting of the miracle symbolizes the kind of charity and unity characteristic of Christian family life and neighborhoods. The Eucharist, moreover, feeds us with the bread of life so that we too like Jesus can give our whole selves out of charity for others. If we believe and respond to our faith, then our entire being, in-

cluding our emotions will be ever more fully redeemed
and transformed by Jesus' body and blood.

The first reading is like a theological commentary
upon the heroic and spontaneous love manifested by Jesus in his emotions and expected of us his disciples. The
First Letter of John put it this succinctly:

> Love, then, consists in this:
> not that we have loved God,
> but that he has loved us
> and has sent his Son as an offering for our sins.

God has *first* loved us, freely and spontaneously, compassionately and therefore emotionally. God did not reason
to his decision to love us and to send his Son for our sins.
Reason, in fact, would have argued against love because
of our ingratitude and sinfulness.

Second, "God's love was revealed in our midst." We
do not reason to the extent of God's love; we cannot measure it with human scales and balances. The prophet Isaiah wrote effectively about the futility of our measuring
God:

> Who among you has cupped in his hand the water
>   of the sea,
>   and marked off the heavens with a span?
> Who has held in a measure the dust of the earth,
>   weighed the mountains in scales and the hills
>   in a balance?
> Whom did he consult to gain knowledge?
>   Who taught him the path of judgment,
>   or showed him the way of understanding?
>   (Is 40:12–14).

God's love too we must accept *on faith,* not that it is impossible to notice but that its grandeur like the colossal weight of mountains and expansive depths of the sea, defies our normal human instruments for measuring things.

Third, God's love implants life within us, so that we can imitate Jesus and respond in ways beyond our normal strength and endurance.

Prayer:

Lord, enable us to love one another as you have loved us, freely, divinely, compassionatcly, not reaching against our good judgment but simply beyond it.

Wednesday after Epiphany

1 John 4:11–18. If we love one another, we possess the Spirit of God and God abides in us. Such love casts out fear, particularly fear of the day of judgment.

Mark 6:45–52. As the disciples' boat was lashed by the wind and waves at night, Jesus came walking on the water toward them and they fearfully thought it to be a ghost. Jesus got into the boat and told them not to be afraid. Their minds were closed.

God's love surrounds us like the air we breathe. The First Letter of John insists that:

> God is love
> and the one who abides in love
> abides in God,
> and God in that person.

This love is so deeply present within us and encircles us so pervasively that we are almost blinded to its presence. We can see an object which is at a normal distance from

us but not a hand, for instance, that rests upon our eyes.
God clasps us so firmly and immediately that:

> We have come to know and to *believe* in the
> love God has for us.

We do not believe what is self-evident and obvious; belief
is different from vision and human certitude. We have
only hints or signals of the wonder in which we believe.
Clasped so intimately by God, we intuit the wonder of his
love.

> Love such as this, "has no room for fear, rather
> perfect love casts out fear."

God's love sweeps beyond our thoughts, reasons and conclusions. We cannot anticipate where it will lead. To face
the unknown ought to incite fear, yet

> perfect love casts out fear.

Love seeks nothing other than the continuous presence of
God.

> The one who abides in love
> abides in God,
> and God in that person.

Even if God's marvelous love blinds us in his presence,
nonetheless we continue to live upon planet earth. The
First Letter of John will insist upon this earthly quality of
Jesus' disciples. The Letter, we have seen already, insists
upon the incarnation of the Word. The Savior is truly human as he is truly divine. John writes:

The Father has sent the Son
as the savior of the world.

Therefore the love of God which abides in us must reach
out to others.

If God has loved us so,
we must have the same love
for one another.

All of us testify how difficult is this commandment
of love. Most of us would prefer to argue religion than to
practice it by love. The rational aspect is always more
manageable than the volitional aspect of love. The disciples of the Lord who followed him in his public ministry
were bothered by the same difficulties.

Even though the disciples had participated in the
miraculous feeding of over five thousand people, the gospel of Mark had to admit:

Their minds were completely closed
to the meaning of the events.

The obvious meaning—of the manifestation of power in
multiplying bread and fish—they caught at once. The
real or the deeper purpose of the miracle—the compassionate love of Jesus for sheep without a shepherd, wan-
dering in their enthusiam, hungry for lack of food—this
perception eluded them.

That night, then, when they were rowing the Lake of
Galilee, it was not so much the heavy wind or the high

waves which made them fearful; it was the presence of Jesus! True, he was walking upon the waters. Without true love they could not accept this person as Jesus—even though he had just worked a miracle—nor were they willing to accept another miracle. They preferred to plan and arrange their life with total human control.

"Perfect love casts out fear." Perfect love is content with the presence of the loved one. Throughout the thirty-four weeks of the coming Church Year Jesus will come to us in many different ways. If we seek Jesus, then the way of his presence is unimportant. Yet his very presence will consecrate each of these ways of human existence and in ever new and different ways we will be able to love one another.

Prayer:

Lord, you rescue the poor when they cry out and the afflicted when they have no one to help them. Have pity on us in our poverty and lowliness. And as your love abides in us, may we be your instruments in touching others in their affliction.

Thursday after Epiphany

1 John 4:19—5:4. God has first loved us. We must return
this love by obeying his commandments, especially the
one about loving our neighbor. This is the faith by
which we overcome the world.

Luke 4:14–22. Jesus delivers his inaugural discourse at
Nazareth, quoting Isaiah Chapter 61 about glad tidings to the poor.

In the First Letter of John the writer modulates in
and out of the theme of charity. This commandment is
linked closely with the other, most important truth of our
faith, that the Son of God became incarnate, truly a human being like the rest of us. John felt that the Christian
was surrounded with all kinds of pitfalls to compromise
charity and the kindness which we must manifest toward
all flesh. Because "the Word became flesh to dwell
among us" (John 1:14), to ignore the sorrows and needs
of others is to ignore the flesh of Jesus and to deny the incarnation.

Once this commandment of charity is firmly established within us, then nothing can intimidate us or interfere with our expression of love. We have "conquered the
world." It is helpful to note that the word here shifts
from love to faith when John mentions the means by
which we overcome all opposition. Faith here does not
indicate a long series of doctrines, only the basic truth of
Jesus' incarnation. If we believe that Jesus took on our
flesh, then we will love others and seek to do so heroically.

In this faith then we have conquered the world. No
matter what difficulty is raised by the world against us—
even if it be as terrifying as death upon the cross—the

world is simply providing an ever more heroic way by which we can love others.

Love as mighty as this is not a recommendation. It is a "commandment." When John refers to the commandment of the Lord for charity, he is probably referring to Jesus' own words (Mark 12:29–31) when Jesus quoted from Deuteronomy 6:4–5 and clearly indicated the first and second commandment: to love God and to love one's neighbor with all our mind, heart and power. Heroic love with all our life's power and endurance is not asked of us everyday; most of life follows a routine cycle of events. Yet when "the day of the Lord" dawns, we must face the terrifying prophecy of Amos:

> Woe to those who yearn for the day of the Lord!
>> What will this day of the Lord mean for you?
> Darkness and not light! (Am 5:18)

We must face this day realistically and heroically. We must be realistic as we have no choice but to accept the situation. We must be heroic for only in this way can we be faithful to God's commandment. It is not a recommendation!

The importance of this commandment of loving others, particularly in their moments of need and sorrow, is further enhanced in the gospel. According to Luke, Jesus inaugurated his public ministry at Nazareth in his hometown synagogue. When the scroll was handed to him, he did not read from one of the normal Sabbath selections but deliberately unrolled the scroll to Isaiah 61. Jesus' messianic ministry was to consist in:

> bringing glad tidings to the poor
> [by means of]

proclaiming liberty to captives,
recovery of sight to the blind
and release to prisoners.

Such was his commandment from the Heavenly Father
and such was the commandment now placed by Jesus
upon others:

Today this Scripture passage is fulfilled in your
hearing.

The passage from Isaiah depends upon an Israelite
institution called the jubilee year. Every fiftieth year all
debts were remitted, all property returned to its original
owner and the land was to lie fallow. Whatever grew was
common property for everyone (Lev 25). Jesus seems to
have taken this beautiful ideal, reserved for every fiftieth
year and observed only symbolically or by some limited
gestures, and turned it into a continuous way of life. Jesus
did not interfere with the rights of private property, but
he frequently transcended those rights by a higher law—
that of charity.

On our part this same Scripture passage is being fulfilled in our hearing! It is challenging our "rights" and
our "possessions." It is interfering with our use of time.
We are being anointed to reach out to the poor, who are
sent to us for care. Each of us is sent to free the others
from their captivity. Normally the need is small and the
demand upon us is reasonable. If we respond quickly and
generously, then we will be prepared for that "day of the
Lord" when the commandment of love will make heroic
expectations. We will not be free to ignore it without destroying faith and therefore being destroyed ourselves by
the world.

Prayer:

God, you so loved the world that you gave your only Son. How can I ever refuse the poor and the needy? How can I ever lose confidence in the care of others for me? Keep me strong in this faith and then I will overcome the world.

Friday after Epiphany

1 John 5:5–13. Eternal life is to possess the Son and to believe that Jesus came in water and in blood. The Spirit testifies to this.

Luke 5:12–16. Jesus cured a leper who had bowed to the ground and said, "Lord, if you will to do so, you can cure me." Jesus' reputation spread and great crowds gathered to hear him and to be cured of their maladies.

In the readings from the First Letter of John, occurring since the feast of St. John on December 27, we sense a circuitous or meditative style. The same ideas continually reoccur. Ideas can be expressed vigorously, for instance:

> Whoever does not believe God
> has made God a liar.

Yet none of these ideas are pursued vigorously or extensively. Rather than say that John's style is prayerful, it may be more correct to call it liturgical, public prayer. A liturgical congregation is united by means of sacramental symbols and absorbs their meaning by meditative refrains. Public prayer tends to soften the prophetic thrust which can antagonize and divide and, instead, seeks to keep the community united in the Lord Jesus.

Luke's gospel impresses us by its prayerful setting. Even though Luke frequently portrays Jesus as the final, great prophet, promised by God, Luke maintains a calm atmosphere. If we compare this present gospel reading with its origin in Mark 1:40–45, much of the direct dialogue and even the indicators of Jesus' emotional involvement are removed. Luke concludes the episode with a sentence omitted in the liturgical passage for today: Jesus "often retired to deserted places and prayed." Where Mark insinuates that Jesus was forced to flee from the political pressure of the people, Luke states that Jesus deliberately withdrew for prayer.

As we come to the end of the Christmas-Epiphany cycle, graced with the incarnation of God's Son in our midst and impressed by the ecclesial or Church dimensions of Epiphany, we need to hear a call for prayer. The Church senses the importance of prayerful absorption of these mysteries of faith. Therefore, we are provided with the coming thirty-four weeks of the ordinary Church Year. Every aspect of Jesus' preaching and activity will be proclaimed, relived in the liturgy, and applied to our daily existence. The weekdays of Christmas and Epiphany have been preparing us for this attitude of prolonged prayerful meditation.

Prayer is that interior attitude by which we realize in faith how God's Spirit is abiding within us and within all the people and events of our daily life. Every word and action communicates so much more than what is said or done, because each event becomes a symbol, like the tip of an iceberg, drawing our attention to what cannot be seen. What is invisible below the surface is much more important than what is seen, yet can be known only by what is visible on the surface. Prayer then means that we approach others with reverence. More than that, we approach them with love because the spirit of God abides in them.

The leper approached Jesus with this combined posture of love, trust and respect. He "bowed down to the ground and said to him, 'Lord, if you will to do so, you can cure me.' "

Jesus' response manifests a compassion that broke through the natural fear of coming in contact with leprosy. Jesus also disregarded the ceremonial taboo against touching a leper and so becoming unclean himself. "Jesus stretched out his hand to touch him." A simple sentence like that makes us realize why the First Letter of John insisted over and over again upon the incarnation. The Son of God *really* took on our flesh in the womb of Mary. With the flesh which she formed into a hand God touched the diseased flesh of a leper. At the same time another simple declarative sentence reveals the infinite depths of divine compassion: "I do will it. Be cured."

Once the miracle is worked, one would think that all the normal processes of life would stop and thousands of angels would perform a heavenly liturgy on earth! On the contrary, Jesus continues with the same human style by which he stretched out his hand. He told the man cured of leprosy to go to the priest and offer the prescribed sacrifice. Moreover, he was to tell no one. Miracles were accomplished out of compassion, not to excite a crowd nor to manifest power. The human emotion of pity or care for the sick was not to be crowded out! We too are to proceed with the normal routine of our lives, yet with compassion so intense that miracles would not surprise us nor distract us from prayerful wonder and ecstatic love in God's presence.

Prayer:

Lord, if you will to do so, you can cure me. Touch my sickness and my weakness, my pride and my selfishness. If you spontaneously touched a leper, you will not pull back from my uncleanness. Lord, if you will to do so!

Saturday after Epiphany

1 John 5:14–21. God hears us whenever we ask for anything according to his will. Because we are begotten of God, God protects us from the evil one and calls us to live in his Son Jesus Christ.

John 3:22–30. John the Baptist did not tolerate jealousy toward Jesus among his disciples. As the groom's best man, John was overjoyed to hear the voice of the bridegroom. "He [Jesus] must increase, while I [John] must decrease."

The difficulties faced by Christians according to the First Letter of John came from what is obviously evil, while in the gospel episode for today the problem emerged from a sincere question about the religious law and from genuine concern for their beloved master, John the Baptist. Together these biblical passages provide us with good directions for the weeks ahead of us, the thirty-four of the normal Church Year. The final sentence of John the Baptist, the very last recorded of him in the Fourth Gospel, gives us the best rule of thumb:

He must increase,
while I must decrease.

Through the increased presence of Jesus we guard

against the "evil one" and the world seduced by evil. Throughout the First Letter of John we do not protect ourselves from evil by fleeing from the world. Such an action on our part denies the mystery of the incarnation by which the Son of God took on our flesh and lived in the midst of the world. As we read on Thursday of this week after Epiphany, we must overcome the world by our faith. We do not beat the world into a pulp nor render it useless in its charred ruins. Rather by faith, we appreciate the presence of Jesus within the world and so consecrate every faculty and power of the world to the kindly work of Jesus.

Once the world is absorbed within the work of God, then another problem arises. Good people become jealous of other people's goodness. It worried and antagonized the Baptist's disciples to see more and more of their group slip over to follow Jesus. It was too much when these people began to baptize as John baptized. (It is interesting to note that Jesus himself did not baptize, only his disciples—Jn 4:2.) When Jesus' disciples broke a legal technicality and failed to wash their hands, John's followers felt confident to press their charges.

We too must be on our guard, lest having overcome the obvious enemy, the world, we be entrapped by the insidious weakness of virtuous people—jealousy and theological hairsplitting. John advises us in his First Letter:

> My little children,
> be on your guard against idols.

"Idols" are all those holy objects, sacred practices and religious privileges over which pious people fight against one another. These things so preempt attention that they take the place of God and become idols! The mystery of

Jesus' incarnation can destroy these idols. It unites us as one family and so removes our jealousy and bitter controversies. The incarnation rescues us by an earthly common sense and we can direct full attention again to Jesus.

Next we find in the gospel one of the loveliest of all responses: joy over the joy of others! How often, unfortunately, joy does not exist anywhere, unless we are the one experiencing it! As we watch Jesus move through the Gospel for thirty-four Sundays, our love for others ought to bring us the greatest joy. It is awkward and unnatural not to be exultantly happy when Jesus cures the sick. John the Baptist introduces the messianic symbol of marriage. In some ways it is amazing that the ascetic John the Baptist, perhaps the most austere-living prophet in the entire Bible, himself unmarried or at least never associated with a spouse during the gospel narrative, makes use of a marital image. Here is one of the finest examples of rejoicing in the happiness of another.

> The groom's best man
> just waits there listening for him
> and is overjoyed to hear his voice.
> That is my joy, and it is complete.

What more can be said: "It is complete."

But John the Baptist has one final sentence before he disappears from the Fourth Gospel:

> He must increase,
> while I must decrease.

As we meet Jesus over and over again in the Gospel accounts for the weeks ahead of us, our love for the Lord Jesus ought to absorb us so completely in him, that we ourselves melt away. Then we will be transformed into his likeness. There is something very healthy even in a natural, secular way about this forgetfulness of self. A self-conscious person is generally awkward, fearful and functioning at only half capacity. Those absorbed in Jesus will be spontaneous and alert, especially about the needs of others. They will be direct and simple, uncomplicated by selfish interests and fears. They will be men and women with faith in Jesus and so will manifest the strongest faith in their own incarnation as human beings.

Prayer:

Lord Jesus, we face the future peacefully in your company. We will never walk in darkness. Through your incarnation you are in our midst and through your epiphany your wonder abides within the Church. Gratefully we listen to your word and celebrate your presence, now sacramentally, eventually in the radiant splendor of your face.

PART THREE

Sundays and Feast Days of Advent

First Sunday of Advent—"A" Cycle

Is 2:1–5. People from all parts of the world unite at Jerusalem where they receive the word of the Lord and beat their swords into plowshares.

Rom 13:11–14. Now is the time to wake from sleep, to cast off evil habits and to clothe oneself with the Lord Jesus.

Matt 24:37–44. The Son of Man is coming at an hour you do not expect.

This Sunday's Bible readings focus on the theme: salvation comes for the least likely candidate and at the least likely moment. To recognize it, we need an exceptionally pure mind, an unbiased heart, a wholesome attitude, a propensity toward goodness. Otherwise the stranger will pass us by, unnoticed by ourselves, and Jesus will be born outside our city.

Our preparation for the birth of Jesus within our homes and lives ought not to consist simply in a scientific study of the Bible, nor in a wily way of being absolutely certain how God must come to us, nor in cultivating a sharp, suspicious eye to miss nothing. In other words we do not prepare for Christmas by quoting the Bible back to God and informing him how he must act in our lives, nor by complying with a series of religious practices and generous donations and then settling down in our security. Although we can predict the exact date of Christmas, nonetheless, "the Son of Man is coming at an hour you do not expect."

An unexpected vision of world salvation is given to us in the first reading. Isaiah 2:1–5 constitutes a high point of prophetic teaching about world salvation. It breaks through the clouds like the peak of the highest mountain, leaving the other mountains lost in the hazy mist. Glorious and majestic to view from a distance, this precipitous and majestic sweep into the heavens does not provide the home where people normally live and work. Israel's religion usually ignored the vision within Is 2:1–5 and delayed elsewhere! At best it pictured the foreigners in admiration at the salvation of Israel (Is 40:15) but more often as interfering with God's plan for his elect (Is 10:13–15; 45:14–17).

Not even Jesus moved beyond the ordinary Old Testament position that Yahweh is the God of Israel who separated his elect people from the nations so they would be his very own "special possession, dearer to me than all other people" (Ex 19:5). We read very pointedly in Matthew 15:24 these words of Jesus: "My mission is only to the lost sheep of the house of Israel." When Jesus commissioned the twelve apostles, he begins his instruction thus:

> Do not visit pagan territory and do not enter a
> Samaritan town. Go instead after the lost sheep
> of the house of Israel.

Jesus, however, hinted at a world ministry, particularly in the parables about the Good Samaritan (Luke 10:25–36) or about the son cast out of the vineyard (Luke 20:15). Isaiah 2:1–5 happens to be one of those Old Testament hints that Israel has a mission to the world.

Advent is a time for peace and quiet so that all of us can detect those hints or signals by which God wants to lead us out of our prejudice and fears. Advent reminds us that Jesus is being born "outside."

Despite the monumental preparation of the Old Testament Scriptures, the birth of Jesus took the people by surprise. Yes, Jesus was born at Bethlehem but outside the city! Yes, he came in the fullness of time (Eph 1:10) but people had no time left over from their selfish pursuits. Jesus evoked the tradition of Noah's ark. "In those days ... they were eating and drinking, marrying and giving in marriage." There is no time to think of what God might do; people were doing it all themselves. Their plans for the future had to be foolproof and thoroughly calculated. The people would allow no interference, no interruption. They knew what their salvation was to be and they planned for every emergency. And Jesus said:

> Two men will be out in the field; one will be taken and one will be left. Two women will be grinding meal; one will be taken and one will be left. Stay awake, therefore! You cannot know the day your Lord is coming.

During Advent we are asked to prepare for surprises and sudden changes. Yet how do we get ready for the unknown? By patience in the quick change of attitude in others. By tolerance for people's words and actions that clash with our plans and desires. By listening. By affirming others in their good intentions and brave endeavors. By believing in the hidden treasures still unexplored in ourselves and in others.

In reading Paul's description of the Romans we may think that there was no hope for them. Paul demands:

> Let us live honorably as in daylight, not in carousing and drunkenness, not in sexual excess and lust, not in quarreling and jealousy.

Yet, there is more hope than we surmise. If people this

far gone can be called to "put on the Lord Jesus Christ and make no provision for the desires of the flesh" then "the day is at hand" for each of us. During Advent Paul asks us to cultivate genuine sincerity and strong wholesomeness. If we stop distorting and spoiling the good creation which we are by God's making, then our natural goodness can be summoned from sleep. "Salvation is closer than when we first accepted the faith."

Prayer:

Lord, cleanse me of my false values and artificial pleasures, of waste, selfishness and narrow interests. Let me be ready for that hour of your coming which will take me by surprise for it will fulfill the finest, most wholesome, yet also most secret desires of my heart.

First Sunday of Advent—"B" Cycle

Is 63:16–17, 19; 64:2–7. Selections from a postexilic prayer, drawn from the heart of a people very discouraged yet refusing to give up.

1 Cor 1:3–9. God's gift ought to confirm the faith that God can always bestow still more upon us through our close fellowship with his Son, Jesus Christ our Lord.

Mark 13:33–37. Take heed, watch and pray; for you do not know when the time will come.

This Sunday, like all Advent, speaks the language of *hope.* Advent forces us to face that serious question: what are we to do about our hopes, ideals and plans? If we are a young woman or a young man, the temptation is to fritter away these possibilities by reckless or thoughtless actions which may cripple us for life. Older people are likely to become cynical, bitter or lazy in order to ridicule what they cannot ignore or to suppress what they cannot tolerate any longer. Hopes are so dangerous that they drive the best people to suicide; hopes are also so irresistible that they turn a sinner into a saint. We need Advent in order to be guided by Church prayer and biblical readings in dealing with our hopes.

Of all the early Christian communities the Corinthian church, to whom Paul wrote the selection in today's Mass, was probably the most richly endowed with spiritual gifts. St. Paul wrote to them:

> In *every* way you are enriched in him [Christ Jesus] with *all* speech and *all* knowledge . . . so that you are not lacking in *any* spiritual gift.

At the same time we detect a note of cynicism or even sarcasm as Paul succumbs to the older person's jaundiced approach toward the young and damns with faint praise. He congratulates them for possessing every spiritual gift *except charity*. Yet, as he makes so clear in Chapter 13, charity is the one gift which makes all the others worth possessing:

> If I have the gift of prophecy and . . . comprehend all mysteries, if I have faith great enough to move mountains, but have not love, I am nothing (1 Cor 13:2).

The people at Corinth, therefore, exemplify the ancient proverb: *corruptio optimi pessima*—the worst is the corruption of the best. Another proverb says that it takes brains to commit sin, and a brilliant mind for the "perfect" crime. A child with the greatest potential is liable to get into the most trouble and stands in need of careful guidance. Advent reminds us of the goodness beneath our troublesome people. It gives us another chance to revive what seems lost. Nothing is more lost than that which we have been criticizing sarcastically. Advent can restore the optimism, vitality and innocent joy of youthful hopes. At the same time it protects those hopes with the mature seriousness of an older person.

The work of Advent is not easily accomplished. The first reading from Isaiah provides us with a prayer as audacious as it is sincere. It rends the heavens so God must come down. Boldly it tells God to take some of the responsibility for the sad blight over dreary Jerusalem during the silent postexilic age.

> You, Lord, are our Father . . .
> Why do you let us wander, O Lord, from
> your ways, and harden our hearts
> so that we fear you not? . . .
> Oh, that you would rend the heavens and come
> down.

The people admit: "We are sinful. . . . There is none [among us] who calls upon your name." Yet prayer revives the purest and most powerful hopes, and we meet lines that are repeated again and again:

> No ear has ever heard, no eye ever seen,
> any God but you
> doing such deeds for those who wait for him.
> (*cf.*, 1 Cor 2:9)

"Waiting" becomes the major theme of today's gospel.

Be constantly on the watch!
Stay awake!
You do not know when the appointed time will
come. . . .
What I say to you, I say to all: Be on guard!

Waiting does not necessarily mean stonewalling for the
next hundred years; nor does it call upon us to stop and
do nothing. The servants whom the master put in charge
of his house waited by doing the work entrusted to them.
Yet they cherished an excitement about the future; they
were ready to hand over the best to the next generation.
Each knock at the door was like a sudden inspiration.

Advent, through this Sunday's readings, warns us;
hopes can be dangerous but for that reason we are not to
suppress nor compromise them. The Lord will come suddenly, beyond our dreams and control. Advent, therefore, advises us: wait, pray, be patient and persevering.
The Lord will surely come.

Prayer:

Lord, let us see your face and we shall be saved.
Look down from heaven and behold this vine which your
right hand has planted. Stir up your might, come and
transplant us into your kingdom.

First Sunday of Advent—"C" Cycle

Jer 33:14–16. God will raise a tender shoot or branch
from the seemingly dead root of the Davidic royal
house. Because God wonderfully fulfills his promises
to Jerusalem, the city of David will be renamed: "The
Lord our justice."

1 Thess 3:12–4:2. We are exhorted to keep our hearts blameless for the coming of our Lord Jesus Christ.

Luke 21:25–28, 34–36. The day of the Lord will be accompanied with terrifying signs. Watch and pray that you may escape the terrors and remain with the Lord.

Advent assures us that Jesus *must* come. He will appear *as he is* and strike *fear* within us. Jesus *must* come if God is to remain just. The promises have been made, and as the word of God they cannot be revoked.

Old Testament prophets struggled fiercely with some of these divine oracles. For instance, God has pledged himself to King David: "Your house and your kingdom shall endure forever before me; your throne shall stand firm forever" (2 Sam 7:16). This assurance is repeated elsewhere in the Bible (2 Sam 23:5; 1 Chron 17:13; Ps 89:29–30) yet it raised very serious problems of faith when the incumbent king was an apostate like King Ahaz (2 Kings 16:3–4) or a weakling like King Zedekiah (Jer 38). In desperation the prophets concluded that God must cut the dynasty down to a seemingly lifeless and useless stump or maybe leave only the roots hidden within the earth (Is 11:1; Jer 23:5). In some mysterious way God will then breathe new life into the dead stump or hidden roots and so

A shoot shall sprout from the stump of Jesse
    [David's father]
and from his roots a bud shall blossom (Is 11:1).

Prophecy, interpreted in this way, shows that good people are not to be victimized by those who possess promised security and special privileges. Kings cannot quote the Scriptures to Isaiah or Jeremiah and conclude:

"We can do whatever we please, because the Scriptures say, 'Your house and your kingdom shall endure forever.'" God will certainly remain true to his promises and fulfill his word, but in a *just* way and in a surprising way. With a deliberate play on words Jeremiah manifested this liberation of faith from the false use of Scripture. He took the name of the reigning king, Zedekiah, and applied it to God whom he invoked as "Yahweh our justice," in Hebrew *Yahweh Zidkenu.*

Promises must be fulfilled just as surely as a pregnant woman must give birth. But the form of their fulfillment remains God's secret. Just as parents cannot dictate the sex and personality of their unborn children, we too must accept Jesus just as he is, on his own terms. God expects us to be patient, obedient and sincere in accepting the time, place and circumstances of Jesus' manifestation to us. Accordingly, St. Paul writes to the Thessalonians:

> Overflow with love for one another and for all people everywhere ... strengthen your hearts making them blameless and holy before our God ... as you learned from us, ... [so] conduct yourselves in a way pleasing to God ... you know the instructions we gave you in the Lord Jesus.

While we wait with faith, we manage our lives with sincere and practical holiness.

Finally, Jesus speaks of the fear and terrifying signs to accompany his appearance. This gospel reading may seem out of place for Advent and the preparation for Jesus' birth. Yet a newly born infant must always stir a healthy fear in everyone, particularly in the family that is receiving it. Father and mother, brothers and sisters, all those in the relation are so careful in handling the child, lest they hurt the tender life. Fear incites people to second guess what the child needs or wants; it is not yet an adult who can explain and argue. Infants cry easily for they know nothing about compromises. Children and especially babies speak the simple language of yes or no.

Advent asks us, in the name of the Lord Jesus, to extend the same delicate and "fearful" concern to everyone. In each person and event Jesus is certainly coming to us, with a presence that we accept without compromise, and nurture carefully, even delicately. The Lord will raise up a tender shoot where we least expect life and the fulfillment of promises. We will cry out *Yahweh Zidkenu!* The Lord, our justice!

Prayer:

Lord, you teach the humble and lead them in your steadfast love and faithfulness. Make my heart humble and obedient, hopeful and fearful, so that I accept you in all your appearances, especially in the way that you come to me this Advent.

December 8—The Immaculate Conception of Mary*

Gen 3:9–15, 20. God questions the first man and woman about their serious act of disobedience; in cursing the serpent who tempted them, God announces enmity between good and evil. Evil will bruise the heel of its conqueror.

Eph 1:3–6, 11–12. Through the obedience of Christ we are all made holy and blameless, just as we were chosen in Christ before the foundation of the world.

Luke 1:26–38. Mary bows to God's will and miraculously conceives the Son of God who will reign over the house of Jacob for ever.

The key to today's feast, honoring Mary's immaculate conception, lies in the purifying force of obedience to God's will. In Genesis our first parents were tempted to eat of the tree of knowledge of good and evil, "which," as God made very clear in his response to Adam, "I had forbidden you to eat!" The second reading from an early Church hymn in the Epistle to the Ephesians moves climactically to the decree of God who administers everything according to his will and counsel.

According to his holy will God wanted to share the very best of himself with us. Not only was his only Son to live among us but was even to be a member of our family. We were to be drawn into the life, hopes and goodness of Jesus so completely as to share Jesus' own divine nature by adoption.

*For all three cycles, "A" "B" "C"

God chose us in him [Christ] before the world
began, to be holy and blameless in his sight, to
be full of love; he likewise predestined us
through Christ Jesus to be his adopted children.

God's will, therefore, can be compared with the compelling demands which goodness makes upon a good person.
An honest person cannot help but speak the truth. Dis-
honesty would trouble his conscience no end till he
came clean. A generous person is perpetually giving gifts
and finds most joy in sharing with others. God, it seems
from Paul's words, lived under the eternal demands of his
generous goodness, to share with us the best of himself,
his word that expresses his most intimate life. God had to
be obedient to what he was "before the world began and
ever continues to be." Such obedience does not consist in
complying with external directions nor in any groveling
loss of personal integrity. Yet it is the most compelling,
non-negotiable demand—to be fully who we are at the
depths of ourselves.

Because we were created according to a will and
counsel no less glorious and exalted than Jesus himself,
our nature is continually summoning us to an ideal far
beyond our ability and understanding. We live much
more according to the intuitive expectations of faith than
according to clear ideas in our intellect. As a result a
healthy tension is always summoning us beyond our best
ideas, so that we live by faith in the Son of God who
loved us and gave himself up for us.

There is always the temptation, experienced from
the very beginning by our first parents, to settle for something less which nonetheless seems very good. In the story of the fall, we read:

The woman saw that the tree was good for
food, pleasing to the eyes, and desirable for
gaining wisdom (Gen 3:6).

Later in the same chapter we witness the inevitable human struggle when people abuse God's beautiful gifts.
They tend to shift the blame to another person—so there
arises jealousy, fear, antagonism, aggressiveness, open
hostility, Eventually Cain kills his own brother Abel!
God, however, would never abandon his children. Goodness will be bruised in its struggle with evil, yet goodness
shall triumph. Goodness shall be victorious in the end,
for such is the eternal "will and counsel" of God according to which "we were predestined."

God enters into this eternal struggle through his divine Word, born in our midst:

It is in Christ and through his blood that we
have been redeemed and our sins forgiven, so
immeasurably generous is God's favor to us
(Eph 1:7–8).

Yet the bruising of the woman's offspring and the shed-
ding of his blood upon the cross strengthens the manifestation of God's goodness and wisdom: "God so loved the
world that he gave his only Son" (John 3:16). "In this . . .
God proves his love for us: that while we were still sinners, Christ died for us" (Rom. 5:8). Jesus was obedient
unto death (Phil 2:8).

The revelation of God's obedient love makes its first
Gospel appearance in the responses of Mary and Joseph.
When Mary was called to be the mother of the Messiah,
her initial response shows up in a troubled wonderment:
"How can this be?" but her final attitude was "I am the

servant of the Lord. Let it be done as you say." Joseph too put aside his first plan of action, which was to divorce Mary privately, and as the Scriptures tell us, "he did as the angel of the Lord had directed him and received her into his home as his wife" (Matt 1:24).

Mary's interior reaction is developed more fully by Luke's gospel than we find to be the case with Joseph in Matthew's gospel. By carefully comparing the annunciation scene with the prophecy of Zephaniah 3:14–20, with the description of the Tabernacle in Exodus 40, or with the account of the world's creation in Genesis 1, we see that Mary was as sinless and pure as the Holy of Holies, as obedient to God's will as the priestly regulations of the Torah, as immediately creative of life as God's word at the beginning of time. Later during his public ministry Jesus extolled Mary's obedience more than any other quality about her (Luke 8:19–21). Obedience then characterized both Mary and Jesus—Mary in conceiving the Son of God, Jesus in dying on the cross.

In creating Mary so "immaculately" conformed to Jesus, she more than any other human being would have been eternally foreseen in Jesus before the foundation of the earth. Mary too submitted to what she could not possibly understand, for God's goodness in her reached beyond her comprehension. It is important to note that the angel did not really answer Mary's question but addressed her faith in God's overwhelming power and goodness.

During Advent, as we prepare for the birth of Jesus in our midst, we celebrate this feastday of Mary which reminds us of the eternal goodness at the source and root of our life. That which we seek this Advent, we have been from all eternity in God's "will and counsel." Through Mary's obedience we are urged to submit in faith to

God's wonderful plans and exalted goodness. Like Mary
we are not capitulating to an unreasonable taskmaster
but to the expectations of what we really are at the base
and root of ourselves. Mary's immaculate conception
calls us to be more freely and totally ourselves according
to God's eternal purpose. The struggle is eminently
worthwhile for victory is assured in Jesus.

Prayer:

We sing a new song—as old as eternity, as new as
the vision of goodness we see this moment in Mary's immaculate conception. God has done marvelous things.

Second Sunday of Advent—"A" Cycle

Is 11:1–10. After destruction and long waiting, the off-
    spring of David will come as a tender shoot out of the
    hidden root of Jesse, David's father; a new paradise
    will be enjoyed by all.
Rom 15:4–9. Everything has been written for our instruc-
    tion and encouragement, so that we may live in perfect
    harmony with one another.
Matt 3:1–12. John the Baptist appeared, a voice crying in
    the wilderness, a threat to the powerful, a humble pre-
    cursor to Jesus. Jesus will gather the wheat into the
    granary but will burn the chaff with unquenchable fire.

In order to welcome Jesus—and such is the purpose
of Advent—we must reach out to "welcome one another." All the readings for this Second Sunday of Advent center upon reconciliation and the conditions laid
down by Jesus. Today's second reading put it plainly:
"Accept one another as Christ accepted you."

The reading from Isaiah announces reconciliation in a highly symbolic way:

> The wolf shall be the guest of the lamb
>   and the leopard shall lie down with the kid;
> The calf and the young lion shall browse together,
>   with a little child to guide them.

We are back again in the first paradise, where all the animals are tame and no one has the least fear or suspicion. Even "the baby shall play by the cobra's den." This abundance of innocent joy depends upon the righteousness of man and woman. Therefore the prophet anticipated the account of the new paradise by speaking of the justice with which the poor and the meek are defended and the wicked are removed. Just as the animals became wild and fearful by the sin of the first parents, the redemption of humankind will restore the entire earth to its pristine peace.

Redemption is God's achievement, not ours. And so Isaiah awaits the day when "the Spirit of the Lord shall rest" upon us. First it will come upon the root of Jesse who was David's father, and from this royal line Jesus will appear. Through Jesus the same spirit will be poured out upon each of us. It will be *a spirit of wisdom and understanding* by which the deepest ancestral norms will give a good instinct for doing all things correctly, *a spirit of counsel and might* so that everyone will immediately manifest strength of conscience and integral goodness toward everyone else, *a spirit of knowledge and fear of the Lord* by which the wonder of God's good judgment will be spread abroad. There will be *delight* everywhere.

Such spontaneous goodness in the human family may seem to us as impossible as the desert's blooming with luxuriant growth. Yet deserts do come to life miraculously! In today's Holy Land a person can tramp through the deep cleft of the wadi el Qilt that cuts through the wilderness of Judea east of Jerusalem and come suddenly upon beautiful manifestations of life. A single stalk grows out of the baked rocky terrain, reaches one to three feet toward heaven, without a single leaf for that would mean the loss of moisture, and then it breaks into bloom. Its root or bulb, protected by its highly poisonous texture, retains its moisture for months before this season of growth. This same stretch of mountains that quickly collapses to 1,300 feet below sea level at Jericho can suddenly, overnight, be swept with grass after a rare torrential downpour. Isaiah spoke of such a miraculous moment when the Spirit—the Hebrew word can also mean the wind which brings dew and rain—rests upon the root of Jesse and a shoot comes forth.

This Advent we wait, like the wilderness of Judea, for the Spirit of the Lord to rest upon us so that the depth of life—life of innate goodness and integrity, of wisdom and sound judgment—will blossom. In this our transformation the planet earth will no longer be abused with waste and pollution. Wild animals will learn to trust and obey.

In his letter to the Romans St. Paul gathers these ideas together less symbolically, more theoretically. He is principally concerned with the reconciliation of gentiles and Jews in Christ Jesus. How this will happen remains for Paul the most profound "mystery" (Rom 11:25). Yet he will settle for nothing less than a new human family; he presents his tableau of paradise in Chapter 8 of this epistle, in which "creation groans and is in agony" as it awaits "the glorious freedom [and redemption] of the children of God" (Rom 8:21–22). We are called to begin this assembly of all God's children this Advent as "we accept one another" and "live in perfect harmony" with people ever more distant, different and even hostile to us.

If we refuse, then we will face the stern and uncompromising John the Baptist who is a "voice crying in the wilderness: prepare the way of the Lord." He demanded: "Give some evidence that you mean to reform." Or else "the axe is laid to the root . . . [and the tree] will be cut down and thrown into the fire." If we argue that the person whom we reject cannot change and be reconciled, John replies: "God can raise up children to Abraham from those very stones." The desert can and will blossom again. This Advent we make the decision whether we will belong to the new paradise; the decision is made by our outreach for reconciliation.

Prayer:

Lord, you promise to pity the weak and strengthen the needy. Pity me, for I feel too weak to seek reconciliation. Break down my barriers to forgiveness so that your dominion will extend from sea to sea and from the River to the end of the earth.

Second Sunday of Advent—"B" Cycle

Is 40:1–5, 9–11. From his heavenly court God summons angels to comfort his people and a prophet to prepare the way of the Lord. The people will return to the Holy City, manifesting God's wondrous presence in their midst.

2 Peter 3:8–14. When the early Church was confused over the delay of Christ's second coming and the transformation of the universe, people were advised to persevere in their waiting and to seek after holiness and godliness.

Mark 1:1–8. This gospel begins abruptly with John the Baptist who immediately stepped aside for Jesus, the one who would baptize with the Holy Spirit.

Mark is the only evangelist who introduces the word "Gospel" in his opening statement: "The beginning of the *Gospel* of Jesus Christ, the Son of God." The passage from Isaiah 40, moreover, turns out to be the most prominent use of the same word, Gospel, in the Old Testament. Translated from the Hebrew, *mebassereth* reads "herald of glad tidings." Isaiah, therefore, guides us in appreciating the true meaning of a word, that migrated from the Hebrew, into Greek and Latin, to our English form of *Gospel.*

"Gospel" first of all means *people,* God's people as they manifest the glad tidings of the Lord's presence in their midst *or* as they become the instruments of God's redemptive presence toward others. Isaiah considers Zion or Jerusalem to be the "herald of glad tidings." Zion indicates God's people, who are gathered in the folds of his garment the way a shepherd makes a large pocket out of his outer cloak to carry a lamb. Zion is also pictured as the Holy City with the temple rising gloriously on its highest northern plateau. Echoing across the valleys are the glad tidings: "Here is your God!"

Zion then *is* the glorious presence of God within a people redeemed and at rest. Isaiah also pictures God's people streaming across the desert as mountains collapse and valleys rise to make straight the way of the Lord. Nations in awe see "the glory of the Lord." Again people are "the heralds of glad tidings," the Gospel, first of all for themselves but with a hint for all humankind. This Advent Jesus comes in order that he may be manifest in our midst. *We* are to become "the heralds of glad tidings," the "Gospel."

Mark absorbs these ideas into the opening statement of his gospel. The gospel *is* Jesus Christ for whom John the Baptist prepares the way; the gospel *is* Jesus Christ present in the midst of his people. If we may employ a technical word for a moment, the "of" in the phrase, "gospel of Jesus Christ," is considered to be an example of the Greek "epexegetical genitive." The phrase after the "of" explains or "exegetes" the meaning of the phrase before it. "Jesus Christ" exegetes the sense of "gospel." He *is* the gospel. Perhaps a more correct translation would read: "The beginning of the Gospel which is Jesus Christ, the Son of God."

In any case gospel *is* people, manifesting God as Savior, intervening as God's instrument in the work of salvation toward others.

Mark's gospel, as already pointed out, moves quickly and abruptly. The author is too much out of breath from activity to afford much explanation. We turn to Matthew's gospel for the long sermons and to Luke's for prayer and tranquility! Mark leaps from the sudden appearance of John the Baptist to the announcement that

John's successor, Jesus, "will baptize you with the Holy Spirit."

Baptism with the Spirit teems with might and energy, far more energetic than the stern and fierce preaching of John the Baptist. The phrase sends us back to the prophecy of Joel and ahead to the Acts of the Apostles. In Acts the Spirit makes the house tremble where the disciples are assembled. In Joel the outpouring of the Spirit

> . . . will work wonders in the heavens and on the
>   earth,
>   blood, fire, and columns of smoke;
> The sun will be turned to darkness,
>   and the moon to blood,
> At the coming of the day of the Lord,
>   the great and terrible day
>
> (Joel 3:3–4).

These figures of speech, indeed, are symbols, but symbols always mean something. We cannot escape the meaning here of a wondrous, fearsome and total transformation of the universe. Jesus' presence, in baptizing with the Spirit, will not leave a rock unturned till every place is prepared for the manifestation of the Lord.

During Advent we await the Savior who will baptize with the Spirit. Are we willing to accept such a Savior? Are we able to endure such a transforming presence? But do we have any choice in the matter? Mark leaves no doubt. The Savior who is announced by John the Baptist will certainly come—and quickly!

For the early Christians, however, Jesus came, died, rose from the dead and they still could not see the manifestation of "gospel" in themselves or in Jesus. Their dreary, persecuted existence hardly revealed the wondrous presence of God the Savior. Peter wrote his second epistle to encourage them. He quoted from the Scriptures to remind them that "one day is as a thousand years, and a thousand years as a day" (Ps 90:4). The heavens will certainly pass away and the entire earthly existence will be transformed. At the center of this new heaven and new earth will be the Lord Jesus, the "gospel" in its fulfillment!

Some of us are afraid of the day of the Lord, others of us cannot wait any longer. For the first Mark wrote his gospel, for the other group the second epistle of Peter was composed. The gospel must be announced; Jesus shall come. Jesus in our midst—here is Gospel, the herald of glad tidings.

Prayer:

Lord, let us see your kindness and glory in our midst. Then righteousness and peace will embrace. May we be your gospel, servants of your son Jesus, instruments of his salvation to all our neighbors.

Second Sunday of Advent—"C" Cycle

Baruch 5:1–9. The Glory breaks over the new Jerusalem and God's people return to their homeland.

Phil 1:4–6, 8–11. Paul prays for the completion of God's holiness and charity among these, his favorite converts.

Luke 3:1–6. John the Baptist is introduced amidst the data of world history.

While the ensemble of readings for the "B" cycle, Second Sunday of Advent, sustain a strong note of urgency, the passages for the "C" cycle from Baruch, Philippians and Luke take on a meditative tone, more peaceful and trusting. While the "B" cycle is struggling with the dissolution of the heavens and the earth, the "C" cycle is careful to orientate salvation within the sequence of world history. The Bible and the liturgy are not contradicting themselves. Intelligent people have composed the literature and made the selection for public prayer, each under God's inspiration. Both the Bible and the liturgy respect the many different temperaments of people, their wide varity of life-situations, their various moments of agony and glory. With faith the advent of Jesus is seen to take place in all these ways and places.

One of these ways is peaceful meditation amidst trusting friends and a receptive world. The book of Baruch was composed somewhere during the long silent years of the postexilic age by an anonymous inspired writer. In several places, including the selection for today's liturgy, the influence of the book of Jeremiah is noticeable. Baruch, like Jeremiah 31, speaks of a return from exile. For these reasons the book has been attributed to Jeremiah's disciple and secretary, named Baruch. The author, however, also draws upon literature much later than Jeremiah. Altogether he reveals a reflective type of person. The return from exile becomes a spiritual journey from discouragement and spiritual malaise. Meditation upon the sacred traditions enabled the author to sustain hope and to find a rich value in life that was otherwise mediocre at best.

The quiet but heavyhearted style of Baruch relaxes in Paul's letter to the Philippians. These were the apostle's favorite converts and a warm, pervasive joy extends over its four chapters. He writes to them, for instance:

> I hold all of you dear—you who, to a person, are sharers of my gracious lot when I lie in prison or am summoned to defend ... the Gospel.... God himself can testify how much I long for each of you with the affection of Christ Jesus (Phil 1:7–8).

Paul is confident that God "who has begun the good work in you will carry it through to completion, right up to the day of Christ Jesus." Even though Paul writes from prison and is faced with public trial, still a happy confidence and easy rhythm move through the epistle. Waiting for Christ seems to have all the marks of seeing the Lord already on the distant horizon.

Luke's gospel is characterized by joy, peace and prayer. The author looks out upon the Roman world and also upon the Jewish origins of Christianity—with peaceful serenity. This international setting is reflected in a new formal introduction at the beginning of Chapter three. In many ways Luke here imitates the editing of the prophetical books which locate the prophet, like Amos or Hosea, Isaiah or Jeremiah, within the larger political setting. Luke is confident that Christianity occupies a significant place in world history and therefore ought to be closely linked with it.

This device also enables Luke to point out the world mission of Christianity. Only Luke, in quoting the passage from Isaiah in connection with John the Baptist, extends the citation to include: "all humankind shall see the salvation of God." For Luke this line means much more than Isaiah intended. For the Old Testament prophet of the Babylonian exile, the salvation of Israel will excite wonder across the world. What may have been nothing more than religious exaggeration or a literary flourish becomes a serious statement for Luke. Second Isaiah, moreover, has so many of these exultant touches to his poetry in Chapters 40–55, that he was probably acting under an intuition that God intends more than the prophet could ever express. He was sending up signals of something mysterious and wonderful.

Luke catches the signal and emphasizes the universal sweep of Christianity. Jesus can adapt himself to any political situation, so will the religion preached by his disciples.

These three biblical readings mirror the land where Jesus was born. A land that has been occupied and controlled by many different waves of conquerors, a land that has absorbed the archeological riches of many centuries, a land of extraordinary diversity in topography, climate and vegetation, a land where all kinds of culture mingle yet remain distinct, a land of everlasting hills and perpetual hope, a land of mystics and hermits, of soldiers and immigrants, merchants and farmers.

To appreciate the advent of Jesus then we must be quiet, hopeful and ecumenical, in the spirit of this Sunday's three readings. The ancient Scriptures ask us to contemplate the birth-setting of Jesus within our own political setting, always peacefully, joyfully and confidently.

Prayer:

Lord, may those of us who have gone forth weeping now return with shouts of joy. May those who sowed in tears reap a bountiful harvest. In peace may we await your coming, at peace with ourselves, our family and our country.

Third Sunday of Advent—"A" Cycle

Is 35:1–6a, 10. The prophet sees the desert blooming with new life, as the eyes of the blind are opened, the ears of the deaf unsealed, and everyone returns singing to Zion.

James 5:7–10. The patience of the farmer is emphasized. He plants the seed in the autumn and waits through the early and late rains till the crop begins to grow in springtime. Remember the patient endurance of the prophets.

Matt 11:2–11. When John the Baptist sent his disciples to ask Jesus, "Are you the one who is to come?" Jesus answered with messianic citations from the Hebrew Scriptures and then praised John.

All three readings begin midstream. The author of Isaiah Chapter 35 has been reflecting upon an earlier prophecy (now Ch 40–55 in our Bible) which originated during the Babylonian exile. The exilic prophet's words were almost too grandiloquent to be true; they would lead to a great letdown. Yet a later mystical writer would not wave these chapters aside but contemplated them and found in them a source of hope and transformation. Thus the silent melancholic years of the postexilic age were spirited with new hope, leading up to the birth of Jesus.

James writes at a time when the Church is established with its elders and bishops. Yet that same Church does not know what to do about Jesus' prophecies centering on his second coming. James will not allow the Church to lose these hopes by which Jesus will come again to establish his final, definitive kingdom. Yet that same Church has settled down to a long stretch of nameless years (*cf.* Hab 3:2). It has its own ordained leaders and its own liturgy, now distinct from the Jewish religion and the synagogue. The church of James is pulled in two directions, backward toward the life of Jesus and the excitement over his second coming, forward toward its long and structured existence. James advises: "Be patient!"

The gospel passage from Matthew looks back to its roots and especially to the ministry of John the Baptist with a keen sense of admiration, loss and regret. Matthew reflects upon such questions as these: did the Church have to leave behind its Jewish relatives and friends? Did some of John the Baptist's later disciples have to end up, separate from their Jewish roots and yet anti-Christian?

In this passage Matthew speaks gently yet firmly. John the Baptist was the greatest of the prophets, "yet the least born into the kingdom of God is greater than he." Messianic prophecies, particularly in the book of Isaiah, ring out exultantly in the ministry of Jesus. Yet as in the case of all the prophets people will find Jesus to be a "stumbling block." How happy those, however, who do not trip over these difficulties, but meditate upon the Scriptures and show a willingness to follow God's direction at all cost. These will find their home among Jesus' disciples. Matthew repeats some of the austerity and stern dedication of John the Baptist. Those qualities are still necessary to prepare the way of the Lord.

Not only are we midstream in the midst of Advent but this liturgical fact symbolizes where most of us are chronologically and spiritually. We are in between. There are regrets of what we have left behind or have lost. There are rifts and difficulties which seem impossible to bridge or fill in. We are tempted to over-organize our Church or political life or, just the opposite, to throw off any and all institutionalization. We hear grumbling and rash judgments. We wonder if the idyllic poetry of our childhood and youth should not be thrown aside.

Isaiah's disciple during the long postexilic age urges us to hold on to our poetry and hopes. James advises us to be patient enough to wait through the early rains, the winter months and the spring rains, for only then will the fruit of our labor appear. Matthew takes clear, practical decisions yet without being ruthless, in fact with painful regret.

Jesus can come to us, according to the advice of to-day's liturgy, not just in the buoyancy of youth, nor just in the second coming at our death. Rather he is with us in the practical management of daily life, during the in-between period when we are tempted to compromise, bitterness, and moodiness. Jesus comes as our savior. And how badly middle-aged, midstream people need a savior.

Prayer:

Lord, you are faithful forever. You give food to the hungry and lift us up when we are bowed down. Help us to keep the dreams of our young years and to manage the problems of our adult years. Keep us faithful as you are, so that we will welcome you now and especially at the supreme moment of your second coming.

Third Sunday of Advent—"B" Cycle

Is 61:1–2, 10–11. The prophet announces a jubilee year of reconciliation and return. For this he was anointed by the Spirit.

1 Thess 5:16–24. Rejoice—*Gaudete!* Do not stifle the spirit but preserve yourself, body, soul and spirit, for the coming of Our Lord Jesus Christ.

John 1:6–8, 19–28. John the Baptist defended his own ministry but also declared that there was "one among you whom you do not know."

An exceptionally fine movement links these biblical passages together. Isaiah is awaiting the great jubilee year, Paul in the First Thessalonians expects the second coming of Jesus, John's gospel declares: The one whom you await is already among you—though you do not recognize him.

These stages reflect our own Advent waiting for Jesus. At times we form great plans for the future. With Isaiah, we foresee a new jubilee year. All the wonderful designs of Leviticus, Chapter 25, must come true, as property reverts to family and clan, slavery and oppression disappear, debts are cancelled. Enthusiastically, the author of these lines, inspired by the earlier extraordinary prophecies of the exile, Chapters 40–55 in the book of Isaiah, was able to break through the doldrums of the postexilic age. He felt the anointing oil of the Spirit flowing over his mind and heart. We too at times experience that exuberant surge of a new beginning, and our hearts are adorned like a bride and bridegroom with garlands and jewels.

Lives move onward. Yet dreams remain dreams (therefore important, even if not literally fulfilled), and disappointment closes in upon us. We take a more sober step toward the future. We begin to walk with Paul and to reflect upon his words in First Thessalonians. The people at Thessalonica were experiencing "great trials" (1 Thess 1:6) yet they remained "imitators" of Paul and manifested the "constancy of their hope" (1:3). Paul then wrote words about the Thessalonians which must have consoled him greatly:

> The word of the Lord has echoed forth from you resoundingly (1:8).

Not only Paul's preaching but also the ancient Scriptures reached throughout the Church because of the testimony of the Thessalonian community. Strength surged from their conviction that the Lord Jesus Christ would return.

We too survive at times only on the faith that Jesus will return. Perhaps our Advent this year is caught in the grip of "great trials." We may be tempted severely to dismantle our hopes. The least doubt here can be similar to pulling the keystone out of the arch; with the central rock missing, all the other stones tumble down. At times like this Paul writes to us:

> Do not stifle the spirit [of your hopes and convictions].
> Do not despise prophecies [by which earlier generations relived the dreams of the jubilee year].
> Test everything [for some temptations have no substance].
> Retain what is good [because ideals and virtuous people carry the promise of the future].
> Retain what is good [and] avoid any semblance of

evil. [Otherwise, survival into the future is not
worth the effort].

The spirit, whom we did not stifle, draws us to the
prophet, whom we did not despise. We find ourselves, as
in the gospel of John, streaming down to the River Jordan seeking out the prophet John the Baptist. We hear
him say:

> There is one among you whom you do not rec-
> ognize. I baptize with water . . . but he will bap-
> tize you with the Holy Spirit (John 1:26, 33).

The one whom we have been seeking has been present in
our company all along. Because we did not stifle the spirit, the Lord Jesus is ready to baptize us—to submerge
us—with the Holy Spirit. This Advent, Christmas may
come upon us suddenly and we will realize that Jesus has
been with us all along—with us in our trials, in our
hopes, and now in the consolation of our soul.

We had once dreamed, with the prophet Isaiah, of
being adorned like a bride and bridegroom. Now through
the spirit we taste the ecstatic joy of union. We recall
those other words of John the Baptist, actually his final
witness to Jesus before his death:

> It is the groom who has the bride.
> The groom's best man
> waits there listening for him
> and is overjoyed to hear his voice.
> That is my joy, and it is complete (John 1:29).

Prayer:
    Lord, my soul rejoices. You have looked upon your
lowly servant. You have baptized me with the Spirit and

have done great things for me. I thank you for sustaining me in my Advent of waiting.

Third Sunday of Advent—"C" Cycle

Zeph 3:14–18. The prophet composes a hymn of hope for Jerusalem and the temple where "the Lord is in your midst."

Phil 4:4–7. Rejoice in the Lord always ... The Lord is near. Present your needs to God. Then God's own peace, beyond your comprehension, will stand guard over your hearts and minds.

Luke 3:10–18. John the Baptist preached reform within people's daily round of duties and announced the one who would baptize with the Holy Spirit.

Peaceful joy and silent reflection characterize this Sunday's Advent preparation for the birth of Jesus. Zephaniah gives the impression that the long dreary wait is almost at an end. In fact, the prophet's opening word, "Shout for joy," like Paul's still more insistent, "Rejoice ... again I say, Rejoice!" anticipates the Lord's wonderful presence. This tranquil spirit can almost be compared to a pregnant woman, joyfully appreciating her child without being involved in the demanding chores of caring for a newly born baby. There is still time to extend the preparations, and here is where Paul's instructions to the Philippians come to our assistance.

The selection from Zephaniah's prophecy for today's Mass concludes an Old Testament book up till that point mournful and heavy in accent. In fact, the words of the ancient *Dies irae, dies illa,* formerly sung at funeral masses, were lifted from Jerome's Latin translation of Zephaniah 1:15. The mood changes abruptly at 3:14

where today's reading begins. Zephaniah then sings a hymn of the great restoration:

> I will save the lame,
>> and assemble the outcasts. . . .
> I will bring about your restoration
>
> (Zeph 3:19–20).

Israelites for centuries meditated upon Zephaniah's words and sang his hymn of hope. One of these faithful persons composed the infancy narrative in Luke's gospel (Luke 1–2). In the annunciation scene (1:26–38) the angel's greeting to Mary echoes Zephaniah, particularly in its ancient Greek translation:

> Rejoice, O daughter Zion!
> The Lord is in your midst, a mighty savior.
> Fear not, O Zion.
> He will rejoice over you.

The Jewish author of the infancy narrative meditated upon other passages besides Zephaniah. As a result, there came into existence a lovely account of popular piety. It circulated for a long time in the family circle of Jesus' relatives who lived on the southwest corner of ancient Jerusalem and followed the full Jewish ritual. Not only their sacred traditions but also their ceremonial baths and their fidelity to the law of Moses, their loyalty to Mary, the Mother of Jesus, have all come to light in recent archeological digs beyond the Zion Gate. These excavations along with research in earliest Christian documents and in the Qumran scrolls have helped us to reconstruct the history of Jesus' family after the Lord's resurrection.

These facts urge upon us, this Advent, a peaceful spirit of meditation upon the ancient Scriptures, a loyal spirit of attending to our family traditions of piety and devotion, a desire of reliving these days with Mary.

Shout for joy, O daughter Zion!

The peaceful attitude of Zephaniah continues within Luke's account of John the Baptist, especially with the choice for this Sunday's Mass. John does not require any major change in lifestyle. The soldier and the tax collector may continue in their profession, and in this regard the otherwise stern John the Baptist shows himself much more tolerant than other religious leaders—with the exception of Jesus. We too are expected to remain in our work, our neighborhood, our state in life. Yet as we reflect upon the Scriptures and as we allow the piercing voice of the Baptist to reach into our conscience, simple but radical demands are made, not, as already mentioned, upon the external forms of our life, but upon our attitudes and spirit and upon the quality of our work.

Let the one with two coats give to the person who has none.
Tax collectors . . . exact nothing over and above your fixed amount.
Soldiers . . . do not bully anyone. Denounce no one falsely. Be content with your pay.

Advent gives us time to prepare for the way of the Lord by such practical yet realistic reminders.

Honest and loyal people find joy in reflection. The Holy Spirit leads them into the depths of their heart where God and divine ideals reside. Paul enables these silent sighs of the spirit within us to be put into words and shared with others. Each phrase of today's selection from Philippians can be mulled over for hours and it would be no more monotonous than observing the roll of the clouds across the heavens, particularly in the deep skies of the Holy Land. In this country massive forms of white and gray clouds are driven from the western sea, to seek the mountain tops of places like Jerusalem and the Mount of Olives. Here they melt into life-giving water during the rainy season and envelop the Holy City with their spirit. Here they seem to dissolve and disappear for very little of this moisture is left for the desert mountains and gullies that race swiftly down to the Dead Sea, 1300 feet below sea level.

These soft, life-giving, plentiful clouds provide the context for rereading Paul's words:

Rejoice—again rejoice!
Everyone should see how unselfish you are.
The Lord is near.
Dismiss all anxiety.

God's own peace, beyond all understanding, will stand guard over your hearts and minds, in Christ Jesus in this holy place, at this holy time of Advent.

Prayer:

Lord, I am confident and unafraid. With joy I can draw water from the fountain of salvation. I thank you, O Lord. Grant me the peace to continue reflecting upon your holy word within my family and work. Then like your apostle Paul, I can call out to my loved ones and to my distant neighbors: Rejoice—again rejoice! The Lord is near.

Fourth Sunday of Advent—"A" Cycle

Is 7:10–14. At a time when the Davidic dynasty was threatened severely, even with the loss of the throne, Isaiah promised survival but through God alone.

Rom 1:1–7. Paul has been designated to announce the Gospel—Jesus Christ, "descended from David according to the flesh but . . . Son of God . . . by his resurrection."

Matt 1:18–24. A tradition centering in Joseph recalls Jesus' virginal conception as announced through the prophets.

Advent stirs our minds and hearts gently yet deeply. Advent leaves us within our normal setting of home, work and relaxation and quietly asks us to pray more intensively, study the Scriptures more carefully and wait upon the Lord more persistently. As the Holy Spirit reaches within our deepest thoughts and intuitions, we are able to respond with our very best self. Human talents and personal dreams come to the surface, surprising us with their excellence and energy.

Advent, in calmly reviving the best within us, also makes us realize that this "best" is not sufficient to fulfill our dreams and to make the ancient Scriptures come true in our lives. A moment such as this is dangerous, for a person can react with "What's the use? My best is not enough!" and so degenerate into bitterness and frustration—some people even give up altogether and commit suicide. Another person's response turns into "Well, I'll show you. I can manage!" and will stop at nothing to gain control.

The reading from Isaiah, Chapter 7, emerges from a context of public panic and personal loss of faith. Armies were about to invade Judah, threatening to march into

Jerusalem and dethrone the king. He had already sacrificed his firstborn infant son to Moloch (2 Kings 16:3);
the continuity of the dynasty looked bleak indeed. Isaiah
exhorted the king:

> Unless your faith is firm you shall not be firm!
> (Is 7:9).

Ahaz, however, had already decided to subject himself
and his kingdom to Assyria, immorally selling the dignity
and independence of the people in return for personal
protection.

Isaiah was outraged:

> Is it not enough for you to weary human beings,
> must you also weary my God?

Under divine inspiration Isaiah announced that the nation of Assyria in whom King Ahaz put his trust shall
eventually march into your land and reduce it to rubble,
as though the mighty river Euphrates in flood should
sweep over its banks and roar through the country "up
to the neck" (Is 8:5–8). That fact will establish beyond all
doubt that immoral means, though taken in panic, will
eventually destroy the sinner.

God, however, will save his people and protect the
throne. The dynasty will survive. Ahaz' new wife will
bear you a son; this child, Hezekiah by name, will suc-
ceed to the Davidic throne, yet not because of Ahaz' immoral calculations but solely by God's secret and
mysterious protection. Thus the continuity of the royal
house of David will shout to the world: God alone saves
those who trust in him. According to this interpretation,
Isaiah did not predict the virginal conception of Jesus un-

less vaguely and indirectly in the statement of faith: God alone saves.

What we wish to emphasize at this moment of Advent is not so much the terror and fright at Jerusalem during the reign of King Ahaz but the calm and brilliant response of Isaiah. He did not panic but spoke, instead, of "waiting" and "remaining tranquil" (7:4; cf., 30:15–17). Throughout his prophecy he summons his extraordinary talents to write and speak with the most elegant and persuasive style of any prophet. Yet his final word, after creating the golden poetry of the book, was to declare: one survives only by faith! God alone saves! Isaiah employs the finest human style to state that human ability cannot save, only God!

In Matthew's gospel a domestic crisis frightened and agitated Joseph: the woman to whom he was engaged was found to be pregnant. Joseph, a just man, would do nothing that was ever unkind. He would quietly divorce Mary and disappear from a mystery beyond his comprehension. When sincerity and wisdom had reached their limit, God plunged Joseph still further into mystery. At this moment an angel announced the virginal conception of Jesus through the overshadowing of the Holy Spirit.

Matthew's gospel sees the fulfillment of Isaiah's prophecy beyond the scope of earlier interpretation. Yes, God alone saves—even to the extent of Mary's virginal conception of the Son of God.

Finally, in writing to the Romans, Paul overlooks the traditions about Jesus' birth and childhood (maybe he never knew about them) and relies upon the traditions found as well in the Acts of the Apostles. Jesus appeared thoroughly human, heir to the promises given to David. Yet those royal promises were brought to their perfect fulfillment in a way never suspected ahead of time—by raising the dead body of Jesus from the tomb and enthroning Jesus at the right hand of the Father.

Advent, accordingly, is a time to develop all of our human talents fully and quietly. This season summons us to prayer, study of the Bible, gentleness, clarity in our decisions, faith beneath all our thoughts and actions. Yet as we wait with the best of our human efforts, God will take us by surprise with a fulfillment of divine wonder. God alone saves—but only when we have done our best serenely in the spirit of faith.

Prayer:

Lord Jesus, you created our earth to be beautiful, our minds to be honest, our hearts to be compassionate. Come, Lord Jesus, and dwell within us, so that you can absorb our beauty, honesty and compassion into your very self fully human, wondrously divine.

Fourth Sunday of Advent—"B" Cycle

2 Sam 7:1–5, 8–11, 16. David was prevented from building the house of God, the temple, but God in turn promised to build him a house, an everlasting dynasty.

Rom 16:25–27. The Gospel strengthens us by revealing the mystery of God's will, kept secret for long ages but now manifested in the writings of the prophets.

Luke 1:26–38. Through an angelic annunciation Mary was asked to be the mother of the Messiah.

The Scriptures this Sunday turn to mysteries beyond our imagination and our control, in fact, beyond all human power of achievement. At the same time God is asking us to summon our energy and determination, to cooperate fully and then to surrender as God takes us over the final lap. In this process we are urged to activate our best talents and then to allow God to lead us to something still beyond our reach! We are tested and show up very weak, for we collapse where we always felt most in command and most likely to achieve. There we are most sensitive to failure and criticism, there we are least apt to accept help. Now, however, we are collapsing at the point of our strength. How much we feel our weakness!

In the first reading of this Sunday's Mass strange reversals take place. David was one of those exceptionally brilliant, determined and charming individuals. He never failed, even when he took on Goliath (1 Sam 17). He outwitted the Philistines (1 Sam 27; 30) and won the loyalty of the northern Israelites, usually unwilling to be ruled by someone of the southern tribe of Judah. He mustered exceptional loyalty from his soldiers and conquered a city like Jerusalem, considered impregnable for the two hundred years since the first conquest of the land under Joshua (2 Sam 5:6–12). Even in love, David overcame impossible odds to win Michal, Saul's daughter, as his wife (1 Sam 18:20–29). He now wanted to build a temple for God at Jerusalem.

No one had ever said no to King David, and so at first the prophet Nathan replied: "Do whatever you have in mind." Yet on the next day Nathan must bring a negative answer from the Lord. God declared that he had lived in a tent ever since he had brought the Israelites out of Egypt. Tent was not only the normal shelter of the desert bedouin but it was also the easiest way to abide in the midst of the people, to direct them in their wanderings and to move with them along each stage of their journey. Tent, therefore, signified the most consoling security of God's continual presence. No matter where the people Israel may have migrated, God was with them. Yet nothing was more insecure than a tent, collapsible at any moment, never rooted like a temple in rock foundation. "Tent," therefore, turned out to be one of the most significant symbols of God's presence with his people, the very word in its Greek form that occurs in the Gospel of John:

> The Word became flesh
> and *made his dwelling* among us—literally,
>   *pitched his tent* (John 1:14).

David obeyed. He abandoned his fondest dream of building the most magnificent temple in the Near East. At the same time God did something entirely new and surprising. He chose David as king and promised an everlasting dynasty. Israel had never been ruled by dynasties. Not even Moses and Joshua were succeeded by their sons. Israel's traditions were now to migrate (in a sense like a tent) and move from the more charismatic leadership of earlier days to the institutional and permanent form of royalty. Yet, what David thought to be secure about the dynasty—a visible throne and his own offspring reigning upon it—collapsed. God had something else, still more mysterious in mind, in his promise to David.

Surprises reach a baffling climax in today's gospel. Mary is the "tent" where God makes his dwelling. Mary of the tribe of Levi (though espoused to Joseph of the tribe of Judah and of the family of David) bears a child to fulfill the promises made to David. Mary, moreover, would virginally conceive through the overshadowing of the Holy Spirit, the same Spirit which rested like a cloud over the tent of Moses (Ex 40:34).

Finally, Paul reminds us that the Gospel of Jesus

Christ contains a mystery hidden for ages and now manifest through the Christian prophets. God's kingdom was not like David's in which the gentiles were absorbed militarily (2 Sam 8). Gentiles now had only to believe that Jesus had risen from the dead for their salvation. Such faith manifested the Holy Spirit in their midst. They were members of Christ's body, the Church.

This series of mysteries, by which God reverses human desires and even the normal ways of conception, leads us to the mystery of the Incarnation. In a very special mystical way the text of Isaiah comes true:

A child is born to us, a son is given us; upon his shoulder dominion rests. (Is 9:5)

Or again:

A child shall lead them (Is 11:6).

This Advent we are asked: do we believe in the mystery of godliness within us, within our families and within our Church? Are we ready to be taken by surprise? Do we find our greatest confidence and joy when God leads us beyond our control and expects us to live by hope? Are we ready for God to achieve something different than we planned when we have put our best efforts into the project?

Prayer:

Forever I will sing the goodness of the Lord. This goodness of yours, O Lord, reaches beyond my imagination and exceeds my power. Yet you have chosen me as once you had chosen David and Mary, to be the instruments of its fulfillment.

Fourth Sunday of Advent—"C" Cycle

Micah 5:1–4. Not from mighty Jerusalem but from insignificant Bethlehem would come the ruler of Israel; his origins reached back to most ancient promises.

Heb 10:5–10. What was prefigured in Israelite sacrifices reached a fulfillment in the body of Jesus and his desire to do always the will of the Father. By this "will" we have been sanctified through the offering of the body of Jesus Christ once for everyone.

Luke 1:39–45. At the Visitation, Elizabeth declared to Mary: "Blessed is she who trusted that the Lord's words to her would be fulfilled."

On this last Sunday of Advent, we are on the verge of a new and glorious age. Jesus is about to be manifested to the world amid choirs of angels and the pilgrimage of shepherds. The biblical readings for this day, however, turn backward whether to the ancient traditions of Israel in Micah, to the glorious temple at Jerusalem in the Epistle to the Hebrews, or to the priestly family of Zechariah and Elizabeth in the Gospel. We are never to forget that the future develops out of ancient roots and can never cut itself off from this mysterious source of nourishment.

True, the readings, particularly from the prophet Micah and the epistle to the Hebrews, do not present a simple, quick development from the roots to the fruit. Rather the ancient traditions got entangled in all kinds of history till they reached the birth of Jesus. Perhaps, our best example is the olive tree whose trunk reveals hundreds and at times a thousand years of battering winds and interior decay. The center section disintegrates and new "trees" form around the outer edge, to merge again into the wider arch of the "new" olive trees. Between the roots to the fruit we meet the gnarled tree which baffles the laws of life; it has witnessed generations of people, to be born, to live and to die, peacefully and violently. The olive trees in the garden of Gethsemani have stood there silently as the Son of God prayed and sweat blood and as we meditate upon the mystery today.

The prophecy of Micah looks south to tiny Bethlehem, almost forgotten once David transferred the capital to Jerusalem and Solomon erected magnificent buildings in the new city. Here, some three hundred years earlier, David had been born, the child who would receive promises of an eternal dynasty. These promises to David brought to the prophet Micah's mind those other oracles of the Lord, still more ancient, as given to Abraham. Despite the long history of wars with their victories and defeats and finally the terrifying collapse of Jerusalem about a century after Micah spoke, still the prophet announced the promised one, born of a woman, to be a child of "peace." Not by wars but by peace would this child's domain "reach to the ends of the earth."

By looking back into history, Micah uncovered Bethlehem, "least among the clans of Judah," and saw here in this ancient root the sign of the new kingdom of peace—a sign of humility, a sign of overwhelming persuasiveness, a sign of endurance, a sign that people of every culture and geography could accept.

The Epistle to the Hebrews directs gaze to a different kind of ancient tradition, to the temple sacrifices annulled by the one sacrifice of Jesus, and to the temple priesthood brought to an end in the priestly action of Jesus on the cross. Even though this epistle seems to consistently invalidate the liturgical action of the Jerusalem temple, nonetheless, it quotes the Old Testament Scriptures and deals with its liturgy more continuously than any other New Testament book.

It is not unlikely that the strong exposition about the

obedient will of Jesus, by which we are saved, was partially derived from the symbol of the sacrificial animal in the temple ritual. The blood of this animal was sprinkled on the altar and toward the Holy of Holies to symbolize the one flow of life between God and his people. As its flesh was burnt, a sweet smelling smoke rose toward heaven and testified to the lives of God's people ascending toward their Maker and Savior. This animal then made very visible the immediacy and spontaneity with which Jesus united us with the Father and led us into the heavenly tabernacle.

Finally, in the Gospel, Elizabeth extols the faith of Mary in the ancient promises of God—not just in the words of the angel (about which Elizabeth may not have known anything) but particularly in Mary's way of seeing herself and her unborn child totally within the will of God. A woman of such faith might easily be the woman of Isaiah 7:14 and Micah 5:2, giving birth to the promised savior.

Prayer:

Lord, give us a reverence for our traditions and ancestors. Never allow them to succumb into tiny memories and powerless shadows. Let them remind us of the quiet, peaceful way by which you are present with us. Lord, sanctify our wills to live from our traditions, so that through their hopes our lives be transformed.

PART FOUR

Sundays and Feastdays
of the Christmas Season

Christmas—Mass for the Vigil*

Is 62:1–5. A new light shines on desolate Jerusalem,
    clothing the Holy City with Beauty for her espousal.
    She receives new life and a new name from the Lord.
    "So shall your God rejoice in you."

Acts 13:16–17,22–25. In bringing Israel out of Egypt and
    in raising up David as King, God was preparing for the
    Savior whom John the Baptist heralded.

Matt 1:1–25. The genealogy of Jesus through the house
    of David and his foster father Joseph. Joseph is advised
    by an angel to take Mary as his wife, for she was with
    child through the miraculous intervention of the Holy
    Spirit.

As the afternoon shadows gather on Christmas eve,
the liturgy looks back over the long preparation of our
Advent and the still longer anticipation of many centuries of Israelite history. A tranquil silence enveloped these
weeks and years of longing, but the end is at hand. Something wonderful must happen:

> For Zion's sake I will not be silent [any longer],
> for Jerusalem's sake I will not be quiet.
> Until her vindication shines forth like the dawn
> and her victory like a burning torch.

Yet when people have waited so long, in fact so *very* long,
they react in one of two ways at the announcement of the
end. Either they refuse to believe, for they have stopped

---

*These biblical readings are for use at Masses in the afternoon on De-
cember 24, either before or after first Vespers of Christmas. Cycles "A"
"B" "C."

hoping; or they do not want any radical change, for they have made "waiting" into the goal of their life. Most people have a difficult time dealing with success!

The passage from Isaiah Chapter 62 almost explodes with the excitement of a page from Cinderella. The prophet surrounds the meeting of God and his people with the laughter, music and dancing of a marriage festival:

> As a young man marries a virgin,
>   your Builder shall marry you;
> And as a bridegroom rejoices in his bride
>   so shall your God rejoice in you.

Yet a sharp pain cuts through the joyful song. Israel had to wait several more centuries after Isaiah dispatched this invitation to the marriage feast. God remained silent for several hundred years. The Palestinian morning remained so overcast by heavy clouds that nothing was seen of the bright warm sun.

Matthew's account of Jesus' genealogy from Abraham to Joseph moves so slowly as almost to get nowhere. The names have a strange foreign sound; we stumble and delay over each syllable of Amminadab or Rehoboam or Jehoshaphat or Shealtiel!

> from Abraham to David . . . fourteen generations
> from David to the deportation to Babylon, fourteen
>   generations
> from the deportation to Babylon to the Christ,
>   fourteen generations

In the midst of the protracted list of names we even confront "the deportation to Babylon." And if that were not bad enough, the return from exile never fulfilled the earlier promises. Israel must wait another "fourteen generations."

When "the fullness of time" arrived and the bright dawn broke over the eastern mountains of Moab, people shook their heads in disbelief. God has to send an angel to Joseph. John the Baptist must insist over and over again:

> What you suppose me to be I am not. Rather, look for the one who comes after me. I am not worthy to unfasten the sandals on his feet.

Evidently, after many centuries of waiting, people had firm ideas but different from God's, of what messianic salvation ought to be like. Or they simply did not want to change. Or they were afraid of the light.

We too are still waiting—even as we stand so close to Christmas. In many ways the birth of Jesus long ago at Bethlehem can be read like the prophecy of Isaiah. Many generations extend from that moment till the present time; so much pain and agony, frustration and lost hopes have been expended over the years— and still we wait! Yet, we can no more deny the birth of Jesus than Israel could disclaim the presence of Isaiah in their Bible. We must deal with the reality of our hopes.

Hopes carry the certainty of fulfillment, but also the uncertainty of how fulfillment will come about! Paul wrote to the Romans:

> Hope is not hope if its object is seen; how is it possible for one to hope for what one sees? And hoping for what we cannot see means awaiting it with patient endurance (Rom 8:24–25).

The certainty of hopes is proclaimed by Matthew's genealogy: fourteen plus fourteen plus fourteen generations. Every step is carefully planned by God. Through the darkness of waiting there shines the brightness of God's providence.

Yet the light is so bright that we cannot see clearly that for which we live in hope. To renew our faith on this vigil of Christmas means most of all that we accept Jesus on his terms. Jesus will come within the normal setting of our lives. Yet his coming will take us by surprise as it did Joseph. While we wait for God, it is not we who find God. Rather we are found by God.

Prayer:

Lord, forever I will sing your goodness. So much kindness have I already experienced that I am not only willing but anxious that you take me again by surprise. Then no longer will I feel forsaken or desolate. I will know the exquisite joy of hearing that new name which you speak over me: "My delight is in her—*hepsi-bah*."

Christmas—Mass at Midnight*

Is 9:1–3, 5–6. Those surrounded by darkness have seen a great light. A child has been born for us, whose name is Wonder-Counselor, God-Hero, Father-Forever, Prince of Peace.

Tit 2:11–14. The grace of God has appeared, training us to reject godless ways and to await our blessed hope, the glory of our great God and our Savior Christ Jesus.

Luke 2:1–14. Jesus is born and laid in a manger as angels announce his birth to shepherds in the fields and as Caesar Augustus ordered a census.

Christmas belongs to children and to the child in all of us. Isaiah announced a great light which would appear at the birth of a child. That child was born when Jesus came forth from the womb of Mary. A burst of light startled the shepherds as angels sang of his birth. In writing to Titus, St. Paul anticipated a people cleansed of all unrighteousness and godless ways and once more responding to life with childlike innocence. We adults must learn from the delight of our children.

The biblical readings, however, do not scatter toys around the Christmas tree, nor are they composed of fairy tales. If Christmas speaks to the child in all of us, it is not because the day and the feast are childish but because they are close, as children are, to the wellsprings of life. We come face to face with what is most essential, most beautiful and most worthy of our dedication.

The birth of a new baby in a family is not a childish matter! The impact of that moment will be felt for all

*Cycles "A" "B" "C."

eternity by each member of the family. Not only will the child thoroughly influence its parents, brothers and sisters by its own character and temperament, its needs and desires, its difficulties and accomplishments; but the child itself will absorb the virtues and prejudices, the talents and wisdom, the spirit and tradition of its family ancestors.

The family of the whole world converges around the birth of Jesus. This interaction is especially the case for the family of Israelite peoples. Isaiah first spoke of the darkness that had spread over the northern part of the Promised Land when Assyria had deported the Israelite tribes in this area. What was once the land of God's chosen people had been turned into "the district [or circle] of the gentiles" when foreigners were brought in to resettle the area. The Hebrew word for "district" or "circle" (galil) gradually gave its name to this part of Palestine; it came to be called "Galilee."

This land then of anguish, destruction, deportation and foreign resettlement was to see a great light and to inaugurate the salvation promised in the Bible. In fact it was to produce the world's savior! Isaiah centered the promised salvation and the reemergence of the Davidic dynasty in the history of ancient empires. The exalted names given to the child happened to be royal titles, inherited by kings at the moment of their enthronement:

> Wonder-Counselor, God-Hero,
> Father-Forever, Prince of Peace.

In fact, the Hebrew for this passage reads with the rich sonorous sounds of a symphony orchestra: i.e. *ki yeled yullad lanu, ben nitten lanu.* Isaiah was composing the ritual for the coronation of a new king; other such rituals are found in Psalm 2, Psalm 110 or 2 Samuel 7. Again we see how politics and world affairs reach a new excitement and fulfillment in the religious history of the world.

Luke's gospel carried through in this same spirit. He introduced the birth of Jesus by solemnly speaking of a world census ordered by Caesar Augustus. In the second reading the seriousness of the moment is realized by the interior battle for righteousness and honesty:

> reject godless ways and worldly desires
> live temperately, justly and devoutly
> redeem us from all unrighteousness
> cleanse for himself a people of his own, eager to do
> what is right.

A closer examination of this passage from the Epistle to Titus, moreover, shows that Paul is drawing ideas and inspiration from the ancient baptismal liturgy of the Church:

> to cleanse for himself a people of his own (2:14)
> He saved us through the baptism of new birth
> and renewal by the Holy Spirit (3:5).

Baptism brings us back not just to infancy but to lifelong promises and expectations as a follower of Jesus. Baptism gives birth to Jesus within us, Jesus who was born this day of the Virgin Mary.

Christmas speaks to the child born within all of us. That child is Jesus in whose likeness we are molded and whose glory becomes our hope.

Christmas, like a child at the moment of its birth, is surrounded at first by darkness. This obscurity may envelop the world from great tragedies like the uprooting of people and the destruction of hopes, as happened to the northern tribes of what is now called Galilee. This darkness may be due spiritually to sin and unrighteousness, to world problems and injustices. This darkness may be simply the silence of the night as we pray and keep watch—like shepherds in the field.

Within such a darkness a child is born. World events will not halt the birth of an infant whose time has come. Decrees of Caesar Augustus and the inhospitable situation of a cave would not obstruct God's decree.

> While they [Mary and Joseph] were there the days of her confinement were completed. She gave birth to her first-born son . . . and laid him in a manger, because there was no room for them in the place where travelers lodged.

International politics would not impede God's plans. God indeed would absorb them into his message of world salvation.

By the birth of Jesus this day each of us is freed of chains and prejudices. We will no longer be victimized by national or world affairs. While our entire life will be affected by what happens around us—as was the case with Jesus—nonetheless through Jesus we can rise with a new freshness and purity. We possess the innocence and the hope of a child. Yet that child in us is not a helpless, babbling infant, it is our adult self as transformed by God.

> The grace of God has appeared . . . [and] it trains us to reject godless ways and worldly desires . . . as we await . . . our Savior Christ Jesus.

Jesus at Bethlehem was truly an infant, yet Jesus was also

the center of world history, about to give an entirely new direction to it.

This night, in the darkness of prayer and in the mystery of this wonder, Jesus will be born to give us new directions and new goodness.

Prayer:

This night is born our Savior, Christ the Lord. Let the heavens be glad and the earth rejoice. Sing a new song to the Lord. Light shines in darkness. Come, Jesus, and live ever more fully in our lives. Come, Immanuel—God with us!

Christmas—Mass at Dawn*

Is 62:11–12. Zion-Jerusalem is no longer forsaken but will be called "Frequented," because of the swarming number of the Lord's holy people.

Tit 3:4–7. When the kindness and love of God appeared, he saved us because of his mercy through the baptism of new birth and our renewal by the Holy Spirit.

Luke 2:15–20. Shepherds have come in haste. Once they saw, they understood. Mary treasured all these things and reflected on them in her heart.

Dawn is the time of peace, of soft new colors across the sky, of new energy and hope. Where the night sky had been deep and black, or heavy with massive clouds, we now look up and behold the lovely reach of velvety colors that merge into the ever lighter stretch of blue horizon. At night each sound could be a signal of danger, but now with dawn we delight in the chirping birds, the

*Cycles "A" "B" "C."

cock crowing, the scampering of cats and the silent hum of bees and insects. Whatever had seemed difficult and burdensome the night before, now seems bearable and manageable. In fact, we now look on these earlier problems as pleasant challenges! Dawn, moreover, especially on Sundays and holy days, becomes the ideal time for prayer. The peace of the earth calls our hearts to tranquil joy in God's presence.

The biblical readings absorb the light and hope of dawn. The shepherds who come with calm expectation find Mary and Joseph and the baby lying in the manger.

Once they saw, they understood what had been told them concerning this child.

"Once they saw, they understood." This simple phrase says so much that we are baffled by it. We ask, what did they understand?

Because of Jesus the shepherds perceived a new meaning in their life. The dark clouds of night were clothed with soft new colors. They were beautiful, in fact enchanting, for they spread a glow of wonder across the shepherd's earth. Shepherds would never again be despised for the menial trade that easily brought them into foreign lands to render them legally or ceremonially impure. Jesus was one of them! They would never again be deprived of legal rights, be incapable of being witnesses in court; the whole world now awaited their testimony.

All who heard of it were astonished at the report given them by the shepherds.

Because of Jesus, a whole new dignity descended upon them. Yet they remained shepherds in the fields.

What the shepherds announced made Mary and Jo-

seph pause with wonder! Here is the most unusual turn
of events. One would normally suppose just the opposite,
so that Mary and Joseph would stun the shepherds with
wonder. Yet we are told in the Gospel:

> Mary treasured all these things and reflected on
> them in her heart.

Not only what the shepherds announced but the spirit of
this time of the day turned Mary's heart into a temple of
prayer.

To treasure in one's heart means that the mystery of
Christmas is happening within us. The child within us is
caught up in wonder. Christ is being born, not somewhere else, not even at another distant point of time; Je-
sus-Immanuel is coming now in our midst. While writing
to Titus, St. Paul saw this special grace of Christmas
within the renewal of our baptism,

> The kindness and love of God our Savior ap-
> peared, he saved us through the baptism of new
> birth and renewal by the Holy Spirit. This Spir-
> it he lavished on us through Jesus Christ.

Just as the rising sun throws color across the world with
abandon, Jesus lavishes new life within us. What happened at our baptism happens again this Christmas. We
are born. Rather, Jesus is born within us and as a result
all the riches of his godhead come to rest within us.

True, our daily life seems to stay the same, just as
the shepherds remained shepherds! Yet, because of Jesus,
a new dignity surrounds our homes and our work, our
joy and our neighborhood.

Once they saw, they understood. Once we have seen

Jesus, we have understood the true goodness and hope of our lives, our families and our employment. We have been strengthened interiorly, so that we will convince everyone we meet that Chirst has risen like the sun within our lives.

What we experience and manifest will be treasured in everyone's heart but most of all in our own! And as we reread the Scriptures, we will appreciate ever more deeply their meaning and their message. The Scriptures will enable us to perceive ever more fully the new birth of Jesus.. In the quiet of prayer at dawn we reread the biblical words of our ancestors. Like Mary we treasure each syllable. Or like the prophet Isaiah who composed the first reading for this Mass at dawn, we begin to speak in the words and thoughts of the Bible. This prophet drew upon many earlier sections of the Bible—upon Is 40:9; 54:6; Ex 19:6 and Zeph 3:14–20—in order to proclaim to us today:

> Your Savior comes!
> They shall be called the holy people.
> You shall be called "Frequented,"
> a city that is not forsaken.

Prayer:
Lord, we rest joyfully at the dawn of this wonderful day. A light shines over us and within us. The Lord Jesus is born. Grant us a prayerful spirit like the shepherds who saw and believed or like Mary and Joseph who treasured each word and each experience. We are born anew in Jesus; we live by his spirit, lavished upon us.

Christmas—Mass during the Day*

Is 52:7–10. How beautiful on the mountains are the foot-
steps of the one who brings glad tidings. The Lord
comforts his people as all the ends of the earth look on.
Heb 1:1–6. In the final age God has spoken to us through
his Son . . . the reflection of his glory.
John 1:1–18. In the beginning was the Word . . . and the
Word was God. . . . The Word made his dwelling
among us and we have seen his glory.

Like the readings for the afternoon Mass of Christmas eve, these too span the history of the world in a reflective, theological mood. Yesterday afternoon the
genealogy of Jesus divided the history of Israel into three
sections of fourteen generations each, from Abraham to
Joseph, the foster father of Jesus. The second reading of
yesterday's afternoon Mass was drawn from Paul's sermon at Pisidian Antioch where the apostle showed that
every major moment of Israel's life was anticipating and
preparing for the manifestation of Jesus.

An even more expansive and more cohesive grasp of
world history is shown in the biblical selections for the
final Mass on Christmas day. Typical of his poetic flare
and bounding enthusiasm, Isaiah saw a herald leaping so
nimbly across the mountains that only the footprints are
visible. The herald disappears faster than the sound of his
voice! The words are so wonderful, words of peace and
salvation, that a chorus of voices rings out:

How beautiful upon the mountains are the footprints of him who brings [such] glad tidings!

*Cycles "A" "B" "C."

We cannot overlook the fact that the Hebrew word for "glad tidings" becomes in Greek, Latin and eventually English our word "gospel" (See second Sunday of Advent, "B" Cycle). The entire world looks on with amazement. The ruined city of Jerusalem rises from the rubble. Her exiled children are back home, moving peacefully through her streets.

Yet, these wonderful words of the prophet are but broken fragments of what God really wants to accomplish.

> In times past God spoke in fragmentary and varied ways to our ancestors through the prophets; in this, the final age, he has spoken to us through his Son.

The Epistle to the Hebrews continues to reveal the exalted condition of the Son. Through him God created the universe and therefore he is the heir of all things.

The Son receives as his rightful inheritance the new heavens and the new earth (Is 65:17; Rev 21:1), a universe re-created according to his image. The prophecies—like the world we inhabit—remain scattered pieces of goodness, broken reflections of glory, until they are reunited in Jesus.

John's gospel opens with a vision of the Word as present with God before creation. What Jesus was to be in the moment of his birth from the Virgin Mary, that he was from eternity before the world began.

> In the beginning was the Word; the Word was in God's presence, and the Word was God.

In between the two births of Jesus—born from eternity

as the Word of God and born at Bethlehem as the child of Mary—the gospel of John places a titanic battle between light and darkness:

> The light shines on in darkness,
> a darkness that did not overcome it.

Every particle of light was revealing Jesus:

> He was in the world,
> and through him the world was made,
> yet the world did not know who he was.

Each time that goodness or sincerity was rejected, the battle between darkness and light was fought again. Yet, the light continued to shine in fragmentary and varied ways.

This light still shines into our world today in fragmentary and varied ways. Particularly at Christmas, and especially through the reflective readings of the final Mass during the day, all these scattered reflections come together in the glory and wonder of Jesus.

> The Word became flesh
> and made his dwelling among us,
> and we have seen his glory . . .
> filled with enduring love.

When all this light is united in Jesus, the result is not terrifying but warm and life-giving:

> We have all had a share—
> love following upon love.

If this light, however, is left in its broken fragments, there is continual danger that we be caught in the darkness or at least that we wander insecurely and dangerously. We are tempted to make a god out of incidental pieces of godliness which we separate from the rest. We end up narrow-minded, prejudiced, divided and overcome by darkness. Yet, by sharing whatever we possess of goodness, we unite goodness with goodness. Today's Scripture opens our hearts to this generous gift of all that we possess. When we give of ourselves as Jesus did of himself, then fragmentary pieces of goodness are reunited and the glory of Jesus is revealed. The Word thus becomes flesh and makes his dwelling among us, and all see his glory.

Prayer:

Lord, through the grace of this Christmas, make us as generous as yourself in sharing all that we possess. Then all the ends of the earth will see your glory and break into song at your revelation in our midst.

Sunday within the Octave of Christmas—
Feast of the Holy Family*

Sir 3:2–6, 12–14. Obedience and honor are due to one's parents, patient consideration especially in their old age when their mind fails.

Col 3:12–21. We are to clothe ourselves with patience, humility, kindness and especially forgiveness within our families.

(A) Matt 2:13–15, 19–23. The Holy Family fled into Egypt but at the death of Herod the Great they settled in Nazareth. Matthew sees the fulfillment of many prophecies.

(B) Luke 2:22–40. When Mary and Joseph consecrated Jesus in the temple as a first-born son, Jesus was greeted by Simeon and Anna. The holy family returned to Nazareth where the child grew in wisdom and grace.

(C) Luke 2:41–52. When the boy Jesus was found by Mary and Joseph in the temple, he replied that he had to be in his Father's house.

The Scripture readings move within the earthly setting of our daily family life. The first selection is taken from the book of Sirach, a collection of very practical instructions from a headmaster of a Jerusalem school (Sir 51:23). Sirach ranges over homelife, courtship and marriage, over business, travel and entertainment. He even offers a long section on the proper etiquette for entertaining guests or for deporting oneself at a banquet (do not speak so loud as to disturb the music, do not flaunt wis-

*Cycles "A" "B" "C."share the first two readings but have their own specific gospel.

dom when wine is served, and if younger speak only "when they have asked you more than once"—Ch 32).

The Epistle to the Colossians was written from prison (4:3) to counteract errors and dangers in the early Church. The Colossians seemed to have dabbled in hidden or secret knowledge, which was communicated only among the initiated group. Normal Christians, therefore, had no chance of salvation; grace was reserved for those who belonged to the secret cult! Paul, on the contrary, asked for ordinary virtues which people who love and respect one another practice without a second thought. These are the virtues which flow from the flesh and blood which all human beings possess in common but which are shared most closely within the family circle: mercy, kindness, humility, meekness, and patience, bearing with one another, forgiving one another "as the Lord has forgiven you."

The three Gospel readings give us a glimpse into the family life of Jesus. Each reaches a climax by simply stating that the Holy Family made their home at Nazareth. There Jesus not only grew in size, wisdom and grace but there he was also obedient to Mary and Joseph.

Family life must always fit harmoniously within the neighborhood and its culture. In writing to the Colossians Paul told wives—in accordance with local custom—to "be submissive to your husbands." That Paul was reflecting and accepting the normal lifestyle of his age is clear enough from the verse which follows at the end of today's selection. He wrote "to slaves" that they were to "obey your human masters perfectly ... out of reverence for the Lord." Slavery and all of its injustices had not yet become a major moral issue for the author of these lines!

More than anything else today's biblical readings

ask us to be at peace—within our families and neighbor-hoods, within our culture and surroundings. Patient con-tentment ought to characterize our attitude and response to others. It is not right to step out of line in such a way that normal people do not know how to interact with us. There should be an earthly touch about us.

The virtues which are stressed most of all are those of forgiveness and patience. We all make mistakes, some-times deliberately out of anger or spite, most of the time out of ignorance or impetuosity We are asked to give oth-ers a second chance. Jesus would say: seventy times seven times (Matt 18:22). Futhermore, it seems that the fault which children find most difficult to overlook in parents, or which parishioners cannot accept in their pastors and religious leaders, turns out to be the vice of impatience. Almost every other sin can be overlooked and condoned but continual impatience will drive children from the home and people out of the church.

Yet as we read further into the Scriptures, whether it be Sirach, Colossians or Luke, we sense more and more the presence of a marvelous mystery which transfigures our human existence and searches beyond our human control. While we follow our normal earthly way of life, we realize more and more that we are treading on the edge of the horizon and any moment we can slip into the outreach of the stars. Sirach writes:

> More than this we need not add; let the last word be, he is all in all! Let us praise him the more since we cannot fathom him for greater is he than all his works (Sir 43:28–29).

For his part Paul writes to the Colossians that he is com-missioned "to preach ... that mystery hidden from ages

and generations past and now revealed to his holy ones
... the mystery of Christ in you, your hope of glory"
(1:25–27). It is important to note that this mystery is not
to be found outside the normal way of life but "in you."
It is at the heart of everyone and is reached through the
ordinary process of daily life.

Once all of us, even Mary and Joseph, reach this
mystery, then a kind of divine reversal takes place. The
child Jesus, otherwise dependent upon his parents, is
suddenly found in the temple, answering the questions of
the temple instructors, even putting questions to them,
and replying to his mother with words that she and Joseph "did not grasp." This same sweep of wonder swiftly
appears like lightning as Matthew tells of the flight into
Egypt or the return to Nazareth or as Luke writes about
the prophetic reply of Simeon and Anna as they take the
child into their arms. Ancient Scriptures are being fulfilled. By reading from Jeremiah or Hosea, Leviticus, Exodus or Isaiah, we begin to perceive "the mystery hidden
from ages and generations past but now revealed to his
holy ones" (Col 1:26).

It would seem, therefore, that in practicing the ordinary family virtues of patience and forgiveness, we are
doing much more than overlooking the faults of others
and giving them a second chance. We are being introduced to a wonder hidden within them and within all of
us together. As we, like Mary and Joseph, keep all these
things in our heart and reflect upon wonders we cannot
grasp, our spouses and children, our neighbors and
friends are introducing us to God's presence in our midst.
Together we grow "in wisdom and age and grace before
God and our fellow men and women."

It is possible to reread today's biblical selections and
see how the mysteries, hidden within family life, are also

celebrated liturgically. Sirach turns out to be one of the most popular liturgical books in the Old Testament; for this reason it was once called "Ecclesiasticus," or the "ecclesiastical" book for prayer and worship. See Chapters 24, 44-49, 50 and 51. Luke's gospel, especially the infancy narrative of Chapters one and two, is continually introducing family episodes into the Jerusalem temple or is bringing the temple liturgy into the shepherds' field or into the home of Joseph and Mary. Liturgy not only learns its best ritual acts from the courtesy and generosity of the home, whether among the members of the family or in entertaining guests, but the family offers to liturgy the mystery of God's awesome presence in our midst. One of the important words, in fact, in today's selection from Colossians is "thanksgiving," in Greek *eucharisteo.*

Prayer:

Lord, keep us from taking the ordinary so much for granted that we treat the members of our family with contempt or forgetfulness or with a hard heart incapable of forgiveness. Grant us patience toward one another, so that we may begin to perceive the mystery of godliness at the heart of our lives and especially at the center of our families, parishes and communities.

January 1—Octave of Christmas—Solemnity of Mary, Mother of God*

Num 6:22–27. The priestly blessing invokes God's name over his people and beseeches the Lord to let his face shine with graciousness and peace!

Gal 4:4–7. At the designated time God sent his son, born of a woman and under the law, in order to deliver us from the law. Then we can cry out "Abba! Father!"

Luke 2:16–21. All were astonished at the report of the shepherds who had found the child lying in the manger. Mary treasured all these things and reflected on them. The child is circumcised and given the name Jesus.

In the Bible a *name* gathers up and indicates the direction of a person's entire life. Very often a new name is given when someone is summoned to undertake a new major work. Abram's name was changed to Abraham (Gen 17:5), Jacob's to Israel (Gen 32:29), Simon's to Peter (Matt 16:18; Luke 6:14), Saul's to Paul (Acts 13:9).

God's name, Yahweh, is explained in accord with his "call" to graciousness, kindliness and peace. It borders on blasphemy to say that God has the eternal lifework to surround us with the warmth and peace of his face. Yet as a matter of fact, when he revealed his secret name Yahweh to Moses, the entire setting spoke of compassion:

> I have witnessed the affliction of my people in
> Egypt and have heard their cry of complaint

*Cycles "A" "B" "C."

against their slave drivers, so I know well what
they are suffering. I have come down to rescue
them.

When Moses replied to God that he does not know how
to answer the people's question about the name of this
God, he received this response:

The Lord, the God of your ancestors, . . . has
sent me to you. This is my name forever: this
is my title for all generations (Ex 3:7–8, 15).

To invoke God's name upon us is the same as to
confess our faith in the nature and revelation of God's secret life. He is God in order to be compassionate. Such
is his vocation, for such is the name which he revealed
at the moment of the exodus out of Egypt.

When Jesus' conception was announced, his name
was given from heaven. It means "the Lord saves." The
word Jesus is a shortened form of the Hebrew *Jehoshu'a,*
which combines the word *Yahweh, Yah* or *Ya* with *ho-
shu'a* and means "Yahweh saves." The name of Jesus
thus reaches into the mystery of God, as once revealed to
Moses, and declares that the Lord who is always present
is actually among his people to save them and to bring
them into the land flowing with milk and honey.

We cannot overlook another biblical parallel. Just as
Moses' commander-in-chief had his name changed from
Hoshea (salvation) to *Jehoshu'a* or *Joshua* (Yahweh
saves) when he was commissioned to bring the people
into the promised land (Num 13:6), so too the name of
Jehoshu'a or Jesus is given to Mary's child at the beginning of his life. Like his predecessor Joshua, Jesus' lifework would begin at the Jordan river with his baptism

(Luke 3:21–22) and continue with the spiritual conquest of the land. Much more than Joshua, Jesus would be the instrument by which the name of the Lord would be invoked upon the people and the Lord's face would shine over them graciously.

God's name was invoked upon his people, yet not in the way by which the sun shines upon us from an untouchable distance. God's name rests upon us in the way that ideas develop immanently within the mind and love grows within the fiber of the heart. What seems to be summoned from outside is actually coming from within us. So close is God to us, even dwelling within us, that according to the prophet, Isaiah, we burden God with our sins and weary him with our crimes (Is 43:24).

This statement from Isaiah, in the Hebrew, declares that we have made God a "servant" by our sins and crimes; the same Hebrew root lies behind the phrase "servant of the Lord!" in Isaiah 42:1 or 49:3! As our servant, God became incarnate in our midst and was born of Mary. The full humanness of Jesus is indicated not only by the fact of his circumcision but also by his continual obedience to the law of Moses. According to the prescriptions of the Torah, every male child was to be circumcised on the eighth day (Gen 17:12; Lev 12:3). As Jesus brought the hopes of the covenant to a fulfillment, he shared in the agony of sustaining those hopes through the crucial years of his public ministry.

Jesus' subjection to the law is underlined by Paul. Yet Paul also declared that Jesus fulfilled a still more basic law by the love with which he cried out "Abba! Father!" Again we notice that God lets his face shine upon us, not by a distant enunciation of laws but interiorly by moving us with love to respond with love. Even a very familar, childish word develops within our hearts and we also say "Abba"—the word which is heard all through the land of Israel today when small children cry out toward their father. "Abba" combines a cry for help with loving confidence. Such is a father's vocation and such was God's. Such is Jesus' vocation toward us today.

Prayer:

Lord, as we call out your holy name, we declare who you are, not only in your kindly acts and gracious protection toward us but also in the depths of your secret divine life. We reach lovingly into your heart and receive the strength to be your child, your life, your offspring—to be you! Part of you, your sacred Word, Jesus, was born within our human nature and circumcised within our flesh. We ask Mary to intercede that we speak your holy name with her faith and love. She who is the mother of the Word incarnate is our mother.

Second Sunday after Christmas*

Sir 24:1–4, 8–12. Wisdom proclaims her life with God before the creation of the world. Afterward she wandered the world restlessly until she fixed her abode at the Jerusalem temple.

Eph 1:3–6, 15–18. Before creation God predestined us in Christ as the object of his love and as his very own adopted children. Paul prays that we can be enlightened in the great hope to which God has called us.

John 1:1–18. In the beginning before creation the Word was with God and the Word was God. This Word

*Cycles "A" "B" "C."

came to dwell in our midst and offered us a share in his fullness.

Today's biblical readings come at the end of three different cycles of development. The book of Sirach represents the crowning achievement of the sapiential movement which had produced such masterpieces as Proverbs and Job. Sirach himself conducted a school for young men at Jerusalem around 190 B.C. It was a time of peace and relative prosperity, not a time of tragedy or of heroic greatness. Sirach scanned the normal life of a man or woman at this period and advised the young how to conduct themselves in business or at home, in courtship or in marriage, whether they be physicians or teachers. Yet Sirach came up against the mystery of life, even when everything seemed well ordered and under control. Toward the end of one major part of his book he wrote:

Lift up your voices to glorify the Lord,
    though he is still beyond your power to praise;
Extol him with renewed strength,
    and weary not, though you cannot reach the
      end:
For who can see him and describe him?
    Or who can praise him as he is? (Sir 43:31–33).

Today's selection from Sirach, from the center of his book, reaches back before creation in order to appreciate the wondrous mystery by which God directs human life. While Sirach, therefore, had begun with the normal, routine facts of daily life, he found beneath them an overwhelming mystery by which God is directing us to goals and ideals beyond our imagination and control.

Paul's letter to the Ephesians dates to the end of the

apostle's career. In fact, some scholars think that it is a collection made by a disciple of Paul from the master's letters or possibly from his ideas and attitude. After all the earthly journeys and human efforts, Paul or his disciple had to admit that there is a mysterious hand of God, controlling everything and leading to a goal beyond comprehension and direction. In no better way could one explain God's overwhelming love and free choice of Jesus' disciples than by stating the existence of this goodness with God before creation—therefore before anyone had the least chance to do anything to deserve it.

John's gospel is commonly admitted to belong to the very end of the apostolic era. It is the last of the Four Gospels to be written and represents not only the most serious theological effort to explain the meaning of Jesus but also mirrors the Church with its liturgy and sacraments as distinctly separate from Judaism. John's gospel, therefore, most clearly presents Jesus in the glory of his divinity. He who was first known simply as the child of Mary from Nazareth in Galilee is now appreciated as son of God in the bosom of the Holy Trinity.

> In the beginning was the Word,
> the Word was in God's presence,
> and the Word was God.

John is also conscious of the struggle between light and darkness, even of jealousy from the disciples of John the Baptist. Yet most of all in this prologue to his gospel John remains in utter amazement that Jesus who was the Word with God from all eternity should make his abode in our midst, manifest to us his glory and share with us his love and wisdom. That which makes Jesus the Word of God is spoken in our hearts; that which directed Jesus from heaven to earth and back again to the bosom of the Father is now leading us forward. So wonderful—and so mysterious—is our life.

All three readings, moreover, give an important place to the Church. In Sirach, wisdom is restless till it comes to abide at the Jerusalem temple. Paul's letter to the Ephesians incorporates an early Church hymn, and John is continually linking the events of Jesus' life with the sacraments of the Church. We are given a strong reminder that only by persevering within the Church can we arrive at any profound though still fragmentary appreciation of Jesus. By the circle of liturgical readings at church services, by the comprehensive way of uniting all the mysteries in relation to one another and by the long tradition of saints and scholars, the Church enables us to see over and over again the wonder of divine providence and to celebrate this wonder in the sacraments of Jesus' presence and redemptive power.

We are about to end the Christmas season and begin the series of Sundays that extend from the first to the thirty-fourth, up to the end of November. As with Sirach our reflections will move in and out of our daily life and its routine questions. Today's readings remind us at the beginning that a tremendous mystery lies beneath these surface details of life. If we respond with faith, we will reach what God has lovingly planned for us at the beginning in Jesus.

It is fearful yet wonderful to remember that beneath the most ordinary actions of daily life there is an overwhelming mystery. This astounding relationship of our least actions with Jesus' love and wisdom imparts a dignity to all that we say or do. Everything is part of the fullness that is Jesus, the Word of God, incarnate in our midst. The Church in her liturgy will celebrate all the moments of our life, for this life is Jesus.

Prayer:

Lord, help me to realize that you reach out to touch others when I am kind to them and that you are expressing your love or forgiveness when I speak. Grant me the faith to hear your word in the speech of others and to listen attentively, to see you in others who are suffering or who are blessed with achievement. In this way the mystery of the incarnation, celebrated this Christmas, will direct me into the weeks of this new year and manifest Jesus, your Word.

January 6—Epiphany*

Is 60:1–6. Gentiles come from distant places, attracted by the splendor of Jerusalem, bringing gifts and tenderly carrying the sons and daughters of the Holy City.

Eph 3:2–3, 5–6. Paul preaches the mystery, hidden from all eternity, that in Jesus gentiles are co-heirs with Jews.

Matt 2:1–12. The Magi come with gifts, seeking the King of the Jews, and upset Herod and all Jerusalem.

Epiphany is the origin of gift giving at Christmas time. Gifts bring many happy surprises but they also raise many problems. If we receive a card or gift, we begin to ask if we ourselves have also sent our card or offered our gift! Once we receive a gift, the giver necessarily draws closer to our family and circle of friends. The giver can now make demands upon us as any member of a family feels capable of doing.

These few observations from our own daily life can

*Cycles "A" "B" "C."

help to understand why Herod and all Jerusalem are said to be upset at the arrival of the Magi. Foreigners were drawing ever closer to the center of Jewish life. They were also indicating that this center is not to be located in any earthly king, not even in any particular place of this earth, but only in God. Wherever God's children were to be found, there God was present. The coming of the gift-bearing foreigners then made Herod very fearful. This fact also put Jerusalem on the alert. Because of these foreigners, the life of Jerusalem would develop in a new way.

Matthew's gospel also speaks of the strange way that the Magi are brought to Jerusalem—by dreams and stars. We too have to admit that new friends come into our lives in most surprising ways. By a chance encounter, say on a bus or at a party, a man or woman comes into the life of another and will eventually be the husband or wife, son-in-law or daughter-in-law. . . . We never know what surprises God intends for us as we turn the corner! Gifts can be wonderful in their generous hopes, fearful in their personal demands.

As we reread the prophecy of Isaiah for today's Mass, we are amazed at the gifts which gentiles are bringing to Jerusalem. They are tenderly carrying the sons and daughters of Israel! They are returning home the finest part of Israel, their children, their hopes, the fruit of their joy.

> Then you shall be radiant at what you see,
>   your heart shall throb and overflow. . . .
> All . . . shall come . . . ,
>   proclaiming the praises of the Lord.

New friends can bring out the best in us. Surely they make demands upon our time and resources; they come into our family and share the secrets of our life. Yet they also enable us to reach outward, to see visions and to perform wonders. They introduce us to new kinds of music and art, to unexpected joys and entertainment, to serious discussions and profound insights, to opportunities of helping others and of being assisted by others, to new sensitivities to the needs of others.

All this may happen suddenly, yet St. Paul reminds us that God had planned it this way from eternity: "God's secret plan . . . unknown in former ages but now revealed by the Spirit." Strangers are now co-heirs with us, one family with us, our very own flesh and blood, intertwined with us forever afterward. Because this mystery existed all along, but unknown to us, something within us was crying out for this new fulfillment and for this enlargement of our family. This secret, somehow or other, was our best self, in our goals and ideals, and now is realized through the presence of these, our sons and daughters, who have come into our lives through strangers.

What we hardly knew to exist within us, now becomes the center of our concern, the best of our possessions. Matthew put it this way: tiny Bethlehem turns out to be second to none. For this reason Matthew changes the reading of this text from the way it appears in the book of Micah. The Old Testament prophet declared that Bethlehem was the least; Matthew reverses it to read, "by no means the least!"

When strangers come into our lives, as they did to Herod and Jerusalem or to Jesus, they can be our brothers and sisters, our sons and daughters, because of Jesus. These distant people will reveal new mysteries about ourselves and activate hidden resources and talents.

If, on the contrary, there are still strangers in our

lives, people from whom we would never want to receive a gift, then there ought to be an ache in our heart and a feeling that our family is still missing some of its members.

At least we ought to pay attention to those important signals by which people try to break down the barriers between us—signals of forgiveness, signals of hope and kindliness, signals of need and desires. These are like the star and the dream which led the Magi to Jesus. If Jerusalem had known well the prophecy of Isaiah, then it would have been prepared by this signal that God wanted gentiles to be co-heirs with them—that all men and women must eventually belong to one family, our very own!

Prayer:

Jesus, in many ways you are leading strangers into my life so that I may realize your mysterious plan for me. I will then be led to recognize the best about myself when you enable me to see the vision of goodness in others. Give me a humble heart, open to receive gifts from others and to receive others into my heart. I will then learn that they are my sons and daughters, my brothers and sisters.

Sunday after January 6—Baptism of the Lord*

Is 42:1–4, 6–7. In this first song of the Suffering Servant within the prophecy of Isaiah, God summons his chosen one to bring forth justice to the nations, quietly, considerately.

Acts 10:34–38. To instruct one of the first gentile converts, Peter began with Jesus' baptism by John the Baptist when he was anointed with the Holy Spirit and with power.

"A" Matt 3:13–17. "B" Mark 1:7–11. "C" Luke 3:15–16, 21–22. Three gospel accounts of Jesus' baptism.

We can never overestimate the importance of John the Baptist. All Four Gospels begin the public ministry of Jesus with the preaching of this prophet. The early catechetical sermons in the *Acts of the Apostles*, like the choice for today's second reading, point out the pivotal role of John the Baptist, in leading God's people from their ancestral hopes and promises to fulfillment in Jesus.

Christianity was not intended by God to be a religion distinct from its parent and source. Rather it was to remain Judaism in the latter's full and final development. For this reason the New Testament can never be understood with depth unless in relation to the Old Testament. As a matter of fact for an important period of time Christianity had no other sacred Scripture but the Hebrew Bible. Moreover, it never composed its own book of prayers to substitute for the Psalms, which are still the staple of the Church's prayer. Christianity's firm roots in Judaism

---

*Cycles "A" "B" "C" share the first two readings but have their own specific gospel.

become all the clearer when we recall that John the Baptist who heralded Jesus as the promised Messiah lived and died as a Jew!

Today's feast of the Baptism of Jesus reminds all of us that we are—in the words of Pope Pius XI—"spiritually semites." Just as the baptism of Jesus did not cancel out his earlier life as a Jew but brought it to perfection, likewise our own baptism did not eradicate who we were from our natural birth. The sacrament, instead, consecrated our lives with all its potential and goodness. Baptism perfects what otherwise would remain underdeveloped, isolated and frustrated.

The three gospels of Matthew, Mark and Luke, each in its own way, show the development by which Judaism reached a climactic moment in Jesus' baptism by John. Mark refers to the sky being *rent* in two. He alone uses such an energetic phrase. It recalls a poignant prayer in the prophecy of Isaiah:

> Look down from heaven and regard us. . . .
> Where is your zealous care and your might, your
> surge of pity and your mercy?
> O Lord, hold not back, for you are our father. . . .
> Why do you let us wander, O Lord, from your
> ways? . . . .
> Oh, that you would *rend the heavens* and come
> down, with the mountains quaking before you
> (Is 63:15–19).

Anxious and passionate longing forged this prayer from tears and groans. The same compelling desire for God's kingdom of justice and goodness sent throngs of people in the days of Jesus toward the River Jordan to be baptized by John. For satisfying these finest hopes

John pointed to Jesus: "Behold the lamb of God!" Mark's gospel centers with full attention on Jesus, so that we are right beside Jesus at his baptism as the voice says: "*You* are my beloved Son. *On you* my favor rests."

Matthew's gospel moves some distance away from Jesus and speaks *about* him: "This is my beloved Son." Throughout his gospel Matthew is always explaining the deeper meaning of Jesus' life and ministry, ranging much more widely through the Old Testament and dividing his gospel into great discourses. An essential part of the early Church's program for baptism lay in careful catechetical lessons, ending up in the all night vigil before Easter.

Luke for his part stresses the presence of the Holy Spirit and the almost stunned reaction of ecstatic prayer. He alone in recounting Jesus' baptism states with emphasis, "Jesus was *at prayer* after likewise being baptized." With Luke we have moved away from study about Jesus to contemplative union with him as a voice from heaven is heard to say, "*You* are my beloved Son. *On you* my favor rests." Christianity is not to be identified with correct doctrine about Jesus; teaching is intended to lead us into a mystery of life that reaches into our deepest hopes in the person of Jesus.

This actualization of the best within us and this forging of family bonds with others at their best, this overwhelming awareness that we are Jesus because Jesus is that closely united with us, this grace of baptism was intimated by the prophet Isaiah in composing the first Song of the Suffering Servant. What the Servant brings to the nations—calmly and respectfully—answers their longing and brings their desires to fulfillment before their very eyes:

> . . . my servant
> not crying out, not shouting, . . .

a bruised reed he shall not break, . . .
the coastlands are waiting for his teaching.

"Waiting" implies the expectation of a pregnant woman; she possesses what she hopes for!

Baptism then makes hope a reality but asks that we share this best part of ourselves within the world family of Jesus' disciples.

Prayer:

Lord Jesus, we end our Christmas season by celebrating our rebirth in baptism. We enjoy what prophets and kings longed to see. Help us during this new year to grow more conformed to you in our thoughts, desires, words and actions. Enable us through the Scriptures as well as through the sacraments of your food and forgiveness to grow to full maturity as your disciples.

Biblical Index

(Asterisk indicates a more extended reflection)

Topical Index

232